P9-CJN-305

LIVE YOUR DREAM

Discover and Achieve Your Life Purpose

● A Step-by-Step Program ●

Joyce Chapman, M.A.

NEW PAGE BOOKS
A division of The Career Press, Inc.
Franklin Lakes, NJ

Copyright © 1990 by Joyce Chapman

All rights reserved under the Pan-American and International Copyright Conventions. This book may not be reproduced, in whole or in part, in any form or by any means electronic or mechanical, including photocopying, recording, or by any information storage and retrieval system now known or hereafter invented, without written permission from the publisher, The Career Press.

LIVE YOUR DREAM
Edited by J. Kelley Younger
Copyedited by Ann McCarthy
Printed in the U.S.A. by Book-mart Press

To order this title, please call toll-free 1-800-CAREER-1 (NJ and Canada: 201-848-0310) to order using VISA or MasterCard, or for further information on books from Career Press.

The Career Press, Inc., 3 Tice Road, PO Box 687, Franklin Lakes, NJ 07417

This book is not intended to diagnose, prescribe, or treat any ailment, nor is it intended in any way as a replacement for medical consultation when needed. The author and publisher of this book do not guarantee the efficacy of any of the methods herein described, and strongly suggest that at the first suspicion of any disease or disorder the reader consult a physician.

Library of Congress Cataloging-in-Publication Data available upon request.

Acknowledgments

I want to thank all those whose wonderful books and ideas have helped me to grow, and to invite all those who grow from reading this book to share their experiences with me in writing and help to advance this work. Thank you also to all the "Live Your Dream" class participants who with open hearts shared their own growth to enrich this book. Thanks especially to my family for their unfailing encouragement and for helping to make it possible for me to live my dream of creating this book.

My special appreciation goes to Diane Chalfant, whose knowledge and expertise in the fields of human potential work, New Thought, psychology, writing and editing have molded my ideas and years of experience into the form of this book.

Names and other identifying features have been altered to respect the confidentiality of shared life stories. Some of the character examples and situations represent composites drawn from several individuals who experienced and shared similar stories.

Welcome to the realization
of your dream!

Contents

Foreword

It's easy to get lost these days in the complex jungle of modern life, to become confused, to not know where you're going or even if you're going in the right direction. Are you doing what you really want to do, or doing what you've been told to do, or doing what you think you should do?

Live Your Dream is a book that assists you in defining your life, your vision, your goals. It teaches what you need to do to make your hidden aims possible and how to actually make your secret dreams come true.

Through this thorough step-by-step process you are shown how to remove obstacles, conflicts and resistance. To establish new values, habits, abilities and possibilities. To get the results, support and satisfaction you have always craved. How to let go of being a powerless victim of the past and become a powerful successful victor in the present.

This book was lovingly and compassionately put together by a master teacher who has created a comprehensive learning system that covers all the bases and leaves nothing to chance. It will require effort, commitment and discipline, but if you practice her directions results are sure to follow.

Joseph Campbell said, "Follow your bliss." In her book, Joyce Chapman shows you how.

—Bernard Gunther, Ph.D.
Author, *Sense Relaxation* and *Energy Ecstasy*

Preface

Are you *living your dream*? What would your life be like if you were doing the exact thing that would make you completely happy? What if you spent most of your time doing what you enjoy and love doing the most? What skills would you develop to express your natural creative ability fully? What parts of your life might be left behind if you moved into a fuller expression of your true potential? What negative conditions must be changed? What, exactly, *is* your dream? What would it look like? How would you feel, look, act?

Or are you living five out of seven days of each week of your life waiting to say, "Thank God it's Friday!" Are you putting up with less than you deserve? Do you feel you deserve less than complete happiness and self-fulfillment? Have you given up your dream? Do you remember having one? Is your dream an "impossible dream"? How do you reconcile your dream with what your life is like right now?

We live in the society of "the American dream"—but where do we learn to live our dream? Who teaches that class? What are the requirements? How do you discover what your own unique dream really is? What steps must be taken to get there from where you are now?

This book has been created to guide you in answering these questions. You will discover that you have the answers within your grasp. As you do the exercises presented—and to the extent that you are committed to the process—you will begin your movement toward realizing your dream.

You will be asked to take a close objective look at yourself. You can explore what it is you really want, what is important to you, what your talents, values and goals are. You can build an outline and a picture of yourself living your dream, and gain tools and techniques for realizing it.

As you live your dream, your radiance will energize everything around you. Your shift in consciousness will empower both yourself and others. Your self-expression will feel natural and right for you, and your experience of love and joy will expand exponentially.

What if you really did everything it takes? Could you actually live your dream? Could you have what you say you want? Is it scary? Are you willing to give it a try? Then let's begin!

—Joyce Chapman

1

Defining the Dream

> You are never given a wish without also
> being given the power to make it true.
> You may have to work for it, however.
>
> —Richard Bach, *Illusions*

H OW WILL YOU express who you are, in this lifetime? What is the greatest achievement you can imagine yourself accomplishing? What is the greatest contribution you could possibly make? What is the mark you would make on the world if *you* were in charge of your life—if there were no reasons or excuses why not? What is the greatest *you* you can imagine being? The purpose of this book is to assist you in actively being the person you want to be, and in acquiring the tools and mastering the skills to achieve your ultimate potential.

If someone walked up to you and told you, "You can have your life only if you take a step toward living your dream *today*," how would you respond? Well, life *is* saying just that—each and every moment—to you. If you're not busy living to your fullest potential, parts of you are busy fading away.

In his famous "I Have a Dream" speech, in 1963, Martin Luther King Jr. moved an entire nation to aspire to his vision of freedom and equality for all. Albert Schweitzer and Mother Teresa have inspired the world with their selfless commitment to care for the poor and the sick. Throughout history, great artists and musicians, poets, scientists, inventors, writers, thinkers and leaders have left us the legacy of their dreams for making the world a better place in which to live. Enough dreams remain for you to assume your rightful place among the dreamers—and doers—of the world.

Here are some of the comments made by people in my "Live Your Dream" classes as they began to explore the implications of living their dreams.

I don't know what my dream is. I'd love to discover it. That would be juicy for me!

With a husband and three small children, house, Little League, ballet lessons, PTA and all the rest, putting myself last just became so easy and natural—last on the long list of things to do that I never got to the bottom of. I need to get back in touch with *my* feelings, *my* dreams. I want to have time to work on *me,* so what I give back to my family is *quality*—the best I can be.

I want the magical to be real. I want more than I feel is actually possible in real life. You see, I live this responsible, organized—but all too boring!—existence, with one eye always on the lookout for Prince Charming to come along and sweep me off my feet. So I'm naturally attracted to people with the thrill of great, momentous drama going on in their lives. It's as if I want to adopt their drama in place of my own missing one—a real, rich, fully lived life of my own.

I thought I could find more fulfillment if I gave up teaching and went into business for myself. I thought if I made it to the top of my field, developing a successful practice and becoming a prestigious executive, that would satisfy me. Having accomplished this, I realize that through it all, I've been aware of this little nagging doubt telling me, "There *has* to be *more.*" Now I'm at an age where I thought I would just curl up on the sofa, take life easy and enjoy it all. But how dull! My life is not over yet. I've just discovered I have a *bigger* dream than ever, now. I'm planning to open my own school for entrepreneurs.

It seemed as if there was really nothing I wanted. My house is just the way I like it. My marriage may not be pure enchantment, but it's pretty good. My career is satisfactory—or so I thought.

Then I realized, as long as I pretended everything was okay, I would never have to stretch. I keep lots of "saviors" in my life—comfortable people who shield me from having to stretch. But when I finally stopped to listen to the stillness of what my life has settled into, I heard a much lower roar than what I'd like.

Don't talk to *me* about being happy and prosperous. I have all I can do just to pay my bills.

"I'm so busy living your nightmare, I have no room for any dream of my own!" The moment I heard myself say this to my husband, I knew I *must* take the "Live Your Dream" class. But what an incongruent time! My marriage was breaking up; I was being wrenched apart by conflict and fear, and the desolation of loss seemed all the future had to hold for me. Yet those words jarred me into realizing that for sixteen years of our marriage, my dreams were not *my* dreams, but *his* dreams. I raced around frantically supporting my husband in every rash decision he seemed compelled to make, picking up all the loose ends, trying to make it work somehow, providing the backup to make *his* every wish possible. I finally saw that it was *my* dream, from now on, that would give me the vision to move forward and make a life for myself. I *must* move beyond the nightmare and into the dream.

If you don't have a dream, your life will be about your problems. The matters of "greatest consequence," claiming your attention during most of your waking hours, will revolve around what to worry about next. You can exist and subsist, and you may be tempted to deceive yourself into believing that that's enough to satisfy you. Have a party; play a game; play dress-up; have an affair; the television is always there to hand out a vicarious existence—more glamorous and exciting than the lonely living room or the battling kids. But in the space where the burning desire and the passion for living belong, there is a black hole of desolation, drawing you down into oblivion. Your life force is draining away, as your energy and your aliveness and your vitality discover no other viable outlet for expression.

Once you have a dream, everything else in your life becomes just things to handle. The overflowing sink, the spilled milk and the rush to get off to work in the morning—all assume a different perspective in the light of your dream. They become mere situations to take care of so you can get on with the more important work of your dream. They are no longer matters of utmost significance—your dream is!

People who are following their dreams live their everyday lives differently . . . they walk differently . . . they buy flowers differently— with the intent to be their best. When your life is about your dream, you are always looking beyond. You're constantly striving to go further, to make the most of the present moment. Each problem becomes just a challenge to be overcome, an opportunity made for learning. You will do whatever it takes to get to where you need to be.

When I was a child, I dreamed of being a teacher. I would teach the world from the top of the doghouse in my backyard. At seven, I taught my five-year-old neighbor to read. And I did, in fact, go on to enjoy a successful teaching career for twenty years. I loved finding a way to draw out that creative spark from within each individual.

Once that dream had been fully expressed, I found myself asking, "What's the *greatest* teaching I have to offer?" A new, bigger dream began to take form. I began to ask, "What would be necessary to assist people in completely fulfilling themselves?" At first I didn't realize that the "people" I was talking about was really myself.

I began teaching a journaling class, guiding people to listen to their inner truth, and know themselves from the inside out. Soon a further need became apparent—what comes next? How do you move from self-knowing to expressing yourself in the world? How do you move beyond all the barriers and learn to be the person you want to be? I didn't have a manual for that. Thus, "Live Your Dream" was born.

Then one day I noticed a billboard with the words "To Be Rich & Famous." "That's it!" I thought. "To be rich and famous, out of being *exactly who I am!*" "But that's silly and egotistical," my rational mind said, as it set to work to cancel the idea. However, I had learned by now to honor the messages that come from within.

Gradually, the dream unfolded—teaching others how to be exactly who they are. Let the farmers be great farmers. Let the artists create great art. Let the builders construct masterful cathedrals; let the parents create wonderful children and the singers sing beautiful songs

—all individuals following their own inner guidance and expressing their unique talents in the way they love most, all free to live their own truth. People who are expressing themselves creatively have no need to fight. My dream was about bringing peace on earth.

The dream took on gigantic proportions. To follow it, I decided to go back to school, at the age of fifty-one, for more information and a master's degree in counseling psychology. Balancing career, family, school ("Can I really go back to school *now*?") and a dream. Could I do it? It was no longer a choice for me. Accomplishing and living my dream was my *life*.

Everywhere I offered my "Live Your Dream" class, people were hungry for more. They responded as if they had just been awakened from a heavy sleep, to see before them all their brightest dreams as a reality. They leapt at the invitation to simply "live true to who you are." As they completed the homework, they began to come back to life—*their* life.

As this work continues, my life has expanded beyond my wildest imagination. I've reached heights I never considered possible. I feel more alive than I ever have before. It touches every aspect of my life. My husband and children have encouraged me and have supported this work by sharing their own experiences of the "Live Your Dream" principles with me. It vitalizes and revitalizes me.

Your dream can do the same for you. But its possibilities should come with a prominent warning: This work could be hazardous to your status quo. The changes you make may be difficult, even painful, at times. You may have to let go of things you've been clinging to or comfortable with, to make room for your new, expanded experience. In the process, you will find where your passion lies. You will discover the source of your enthusiasm. And as you do the exercises and begin to express aspects of yourself more fully, you will experience a growing sense of inner peace and fulfillment, and a tremendous aliveness and connectedness with *life*! You will become the *actualized dreamer*.

Discovering and identifying their dreams is a problem for many people. We are often trained to live according to someone else's idea of what we *should* be or do. The inner knowing we once possessed lies buried beneath years and years of second-best living. And we are taught to be modest, to be content with what we have and not ask for or expect more. We suppress our own wishes and desires, and deny ourselves the very experiences that bring us to life. The truth we live is someone else's, not our own.

> I wanted to be the greatest gymnast in the world—but my parents never took me seriously. And I guess I don't take myself seriously, even now. I'm just an average person. I think my biggest dream these days is to get a good night's sleep.

> My dream was to raise two wonderful kids. Now that that's done, I have nowhere else to go. What's going to be my reason for getting up in the morning and feeling good? I *have* to have a dream.

> Denise had been an editor for seven years. Her intermittent heavy sighs punctuated the air with her despair and disinterest in her job. In every free minute, she could be overheard on the phone, cheering up the sick and troubled members of her church. "What would I ever tell my dad, if I wanted to leave a respected position like this, and go become 'just' a secretary for the church?" she agonized.

> Austin has established a successful medical practice, but over the years his work has come to hold less and less appeal for him. "Whose dream was it that I should become a doctor?" he begins to ponder. "Surely not *mine*! I think I'd be happiest making beautiful furniture in my own woodworking shop."

Other people have no trouble conceiving their dreams, but whether through fear, lack of perseverance, disbelief in themselves, or unwillingness to take the risk, the original conception is as far as they go.

> When I was young, I used to dream of changing the world. In middle age, I've had to realize that maybe the biggest impact I'll ever have is just the little things I do for the few people close to me. The world has passed me by now. I'm too old for dreams.

My dreams? So many have come and gone. But they never seem to get beyond the "terrific idea" stage. Maybe I give up too easily, or I don't try hard enough. There's definitely a gap, for me, between dreaming the dream and actually *living* it—knowing how to get from here to there.

My dream is to make *millions* as a trial lawyer. But the truth is, I wear a uniform that says I'm a bell captain.

Still others have doggedly pursued yesterday's dream, neglecting to see that it has died, and should have been peacefully buried long ago.

I don't like what I do, but it's the only thing I know . . ."

. . . only fifteen years to go 'til retirement. . . . I'll just bide my time and build up the benefits. I'd lose too much if I considered changing jobs now.

I still keep hoping someday my husband will change and become the person who can make me happy.

If you're still hanging on to a dead dream of yesterday, laying flowers on its grave by the hour, you cannot be planting the seeds for a new dream to grow today. So take a look at whatever blocks you may have to doing what you really want to do. Write them down, and study each one. Is it worth selling your soul for? Really consider what's at stake. It's your life, and you choose it, minute to minute to minute.

Unlike goals, which are set in place fairly logically, your dream can only come from deep within. When I was teaching small children, I would make a point of asking, "What do you think is the best way for you to learn this?" The child would *always* tell me. Inside themselves, all children naturally have direction. We are not born without direction. All we have to do is bring it forth. You can let that direction and that dream surface, take shape and attain clarity in your mind's eye. The exercises in this chapter are designed to trigger associations and guide you to your inner knowing of exactly what your dream is.

Your dream may peek shyly through a crack in your awareness

at first, or it may present itself boldly and dramatically. Your challenge will be to pay attention to the messages you receive from your inner guidance.

My daughter-in-law Kathy, in her first "Live Your Dream" class, shared: "There's a tiny thought inside me—you'd probably laugh—I see myself on the cover of *Vogue* magazine!" When she explored the idea further, she came to the realization: "The times I feel really *alive* are when I'm right down in the arena. I thrive on being a participant. It pushes me to be my best, in a way that sitting up in the stands as a spectator can never do."

Today Kathy is a successful model, traveling in Europe and calling her time her own—also part of her dream. She's enjoying her life tremendously and living so prosperously that she simply smiled contentedly when her mother asked her, "When are you going to settle down and get a *real* job?" Kathy can understand her mother's point of view and appreciates her concern. But she knows that her dream job *is* her real job. Her vision has made it possible for her to make a dream life a reality. She doesn't have to settle for a nine-to-five job and somebody else's problems. And she would never have gotten there without stopping to honor that "tiny thought" that bubbled up from her subconscious mind.

"Don't be ridiculous!" Debra's rational mind said, when she realized her secret desire was to be a minister. "You have all these *responsibilities*. With your husband changing jobs and the kids needing so much attention and chauffeuring . . . and you'd have to go back to school. It's just not *practical*!" Yet as Debra looked more closely at her life, she declared in anguish, "If I don't have a dream soon, I'm going to be swallowed up by the turmoil all around me." She was so used to living at the effect of everything in her life, that to think of being the *cause* introduced whole new possibilities.

What she wanted more than anything else was to live as the spiritual self she was beginning to uncover, where she found peace and inner assurance. And what better way than to *teach* what she loved, which was the Scriptures? She also realized that the times she felt absolutely her best were when she got all dressed up and went into what she called her "presentation mode."

"Where there's a will, there's got to be a way," Debra resolved, as she soon found herself handling what had been a full-time load in half the time, with surprisingly ample energy left over for her classes.

When you take a picture of your life, focus the camera clearly on its central subject—your dream. Then all the other parts of the picture will come into focus as well.

You may have many dreams, or you may be unsure whether the dream you identify now is your ultimate dream. My experience has shown that living your dream is a cyclical process; no sooner has one dream bowed offstage than the next is waiting in the wings. Working through each successive dream to its completion is a powerful means of honing in on your most magnificent self.

It often happens that through the act of identifying a dream and beginning to build it, people learn something unexpected about themselves. In one of my classes, a shy woman mentioned that she had always wanted to sing publicly. She was given an assignment—to go sing in a piano lounge where members of the audience were invited to come up on stage and perform. She came away from this experience with a positive certainty: "That is *not* what I want to do." It took declaring her intention and then following it up with decisive action to gain this knowledge. Without these steps, she could easily have spent the rest of her life tentatively humoring the possibility, and feeling inadequate and ineffective about carrying it through. The experience brought her instant clarity. Her attention was freed to move on and discover what she really *did* want to do.

Your dream can be as simple or complex as you desire. And like mine, your dream may unfold to greater and greater dimensions as you become committed to it. It makes no difference what your dream is— the important point is that you declare one and dedicate yourself to it.

Your dream is as close as your own mental image of it. How many of us go through our lives troubled by a vague sense that the person we are is not the person we really want to be? But we don't stop to define precisely who that desired person would be. We know what we don't want, but exactly what *do* we want and need? We can easily picture what makes us unhappy, but we don't give much thought to what makes us happy!

If you can close your eyes and picture your dream, you can bring it forth in your experience. Your subconscious mind, that part of you that goes to work creating whatever reality you choose to believe in, is the source of what becomes real in your outer experience. You can learn to direct your conscious mind to plant ideas in your subconscious mind that will manifest happiness rather than unhappiness. You can put your subconscious mind to work in the service of your highest thoughts and dreams. Otherwise, it will continue proving the validity of pessimism and complacency.

The exercises here will help you picture the many facets of your dream clearly and in detail. You can go on from there to plant the beliefs in your subconscious mind that will flower into the realization of your dream. Subsequent exercises will guide you, step by step, to take the actions necessary to bring your dream into being.

As you work through these exercises, it is important to follow some basic guidelines:

- Be gentle with yourself and others. The place where you are right now is perfect for you—look how far you've come! And how well you have been prepared to take your next big step.

- As you become certain of the path you're on, and the person you are, begin to appreciate other people's gifts, as well as your own. Each of us is exactly where we need to be, and is no better or worse off than you are.

- When you don't live up to your dream, just notice what happened, learn from it, congratulate yourself on what you've learned, and move on.

- Your rate of progress will be fastest if you don't waste time focusing on negative thoughts. Keep choosing the positive point of view.

- One concrete step taken in the right direction will take you far. Keep your attention focused, and avoid going off on tangents.

- Practice makes permanent. Practice continually asking yourself, "Am I living my dream in this moment? What more could I be doing?"

STEPS TO PREPARE

The following steps will prepare you for beginning your dream work:

GET READY

Obtain a notebook—your Dream Book. You will be recording many of your thoughts and feelings during the coming weeks, so choose one you will enjoy working with. Looseleaf paper in a three-ring binder is ideal.

Also, purchase a daily schedule book. Look for one that can be used to record and plan your days hour-by-hour. Stationery shops and bookstores carry these in all shapes and sizes.

GET SET

Starting now, do the following *every day*:

- *Visualize.* At the beginning of each day, spend a few minutes previewing your day. What do you want out of your day? Picture yourself going through the day. What will you accomplish? What needs to be taken care of? What will you do for yourself? Visualize yourself living your dream. See that dream as if it were manifested already. What will you do today to advance your dream?

- *Write.* At the top of your daily schedule write, "What I want out of today is. . . ." Write major and minor goals and accomplishments (dream steps) you intend to achieve. Then write a schedule for your time that will enable you to accomplish these objectives.

At the end of each day before you go to bed, look over your schedule. What are your successes? Write, "What I learned today is. . . ." You become the person you want to be by first saying what you will do, then observing whether you did it or not. Your major success for one day may be simply noting that you did not follow through with what you had intended. Be sure to write that down. Do you want to put it on tomorrow's list?

- *Start your Dream Book.* Write to yourself in it every day. Use it to keep track of your assignments and your progress. Get into the habit of using it as a daily log of "where I am today." You never need to show your Dream Book to anyone, so don't worry about people criticizing or evaluating what you write. Just write for yourself alone. Always date your work. When you complete each entry, re-read it and write a short summary statement.

- *Work with a Dream Coach.* If possible, find a partner to work with through the process of "Live Your Dream" discovery. Your coach can work independently on his or her own dream, and you can support and encourage each other as you progress through the exercises. Telephone your coach at least five days every week, and ask an empowering question such as "How are you living your dream?" Communicate your successes and your learning. Emphasize the positive in supporting each other.

- *Read* books and listen to tapes that will expand your awareness and support you in living your dream. Emmet Fox in *The Mental Equivalent* states, "Whatever enters into your life is but the material expression of some belief in your mind" (p. 4). "Management of your thinking is the key to management of your destiny" (p. 14). "If you want to change your life, *you must change your thought and keep it changed*" (p.

22). A list of suggested readings is provided at the back of this book to help you begin re-directing your thinking.

Using these tools on a regular and consistent basis, you will notice your life becoming an adventure, with you in charge of creating it. You will become your own teacher, your own life planner, and your own masterful leader.

Now, begin!

VISUALIZE YOUR DREAM

If possible, slowly read the following section into a tape recorder, so that you can listen to it with your eyes closed. Stop the tape from time to time to write whatever responses are evoked by the questions. Arrange a time when you can be uninterrupted for at least an hour, to concentrate your attention on defining your dream. When you're ready, begin!

Sit down with your Dream Book in a comfortable, quiet place to start visualizing your dream. What *is* your dream? Begin to picture some ideas about it. Allow vivid images to flow into your imagination. Create your ideal scene, writing anything that comes to mind, no matter how crazy or unrealistic it might seem. You can sort out and evaluate your ideas later. For now, just let them flow freely.

Write in as much detail as you can. Describe your ideas in sparkling sensory images, being sure to include the feelings and sensations they elicit.

Suppose that, for the first time in your life, you have been given the opportunity to start anew, knowing everything in your life from now on will support you in "Living Your Dream." See yourself walking down a narrow path lined on both sides by flowers and hanging vines. You are enchanted by the beauty all around you. Floral fragrances fill the air and brilliant-colored birds swoop and sing. Breathe in deeply and soak up the warm, soothing rays of the sun.

Continue along the path until you come upon a scene that you recognize as your ideal place to be in all of nature. Here you are free of all distractions and responsibilities. Take a good look around you.

Do you see blue skies and grassy fields? Do you see mountains? Are there trees, water, flowers, the ocean, birds, sunshine, rain? Note the colors and details of the landscape, as an artist would.

Where are you? What is it you love about the particular place you find yourself in? How does it feel to be there? What is the one quality of the scene you would want to take with you wherever you go? Relax, and soak up enough of this feeling to last for a lifetime.

[Pause.]

When you are ready, gently open your eyes without leaving your scene. Draw or paint it in your Dream Book, and write all about it before going on. Then close your eyes again.

Now, you feel eager to know what lies just ahead. Gather yourself up, and turn your eyes toward a sparkling light not far away. With a springing step, start out across the short stretch to find out what could be reflecting the sunbeams so brightly.

And just look! There it is—your dream house, perfect in every way. It is in the exact location you would choose, if you could choose any place you wanted. Walk slowly up to it, noticing every exterior detail. What kind of house is it? Describe what you see from the outside.

Now walk up to the front door, and into your ideal home environment. Here are all the features in a house that make you happiest. Look all around, exploring every nook and cranny.

Stop for a moment to picture and write what you see. What is important to you in your home? Where do you spend most of your time? What kinds of experiences will you choose to have there? How do your surroundings accommodate these purposes? What does the *dreamer* in you say you aspire to? Dream . . . and write. Imagine you can dream and write into your life any possessions you like. What are some of the things you desire? What objects energize the dreamer in you?

Describe each detail of your ideal home to your complete satisfaction. Now once again look beyond, to see more of what is in store for you, to fulfill and complete your life. Begin to consider the central purpose for your life.

Imagine walking over to a comfortable chair in your dream living room. Sit down, and imagine yourself in the career position of your dreams. You are making the contribution to the world that you came here to make, and using your unique talents to do what you most enjoy doing.

See yourself involved in an activity you absolutely love to do—you can hardly believe you're being paid to have so much fun! What are you doing? What activities give you boundless energy, and make you feel so good?

Think of the ways it is important for you to be expressing yourself. What is the gift deep within you that yearns to be expressed and given to others? What is the special understanding your unique experience has brought to you, that you want to offer for others' benefit?

How is your work important in the world? What profession do you most identify with? If your dream is to be the best waitress in the world, perhaps you delight in making your service personal—remembering individual preferences, offering single-minded attentiveness to your customers' needs, creating an atmosphere that lets them know they are cared for, joking or chatting with them, or lending a sympathetic ear. How are you making a difference, by what you do?

In what ways does the contribution you make lift your whole field of endeavor to a higher level than anyone else has ever aspired to before? What things do you think of in a new way? What outstanding innovations do you make? What new ideas do you bring into reality? What improvements do you envision making in the world? What is your unique role as a dream maker?

Now imagine you're in a large auditorium. Someone walks up to you with a microphone and asks you, "What do you absolutely know, right at this moment in your life, that makes you sure the dream you have envisioned is a possibility for your future? What is the greatest strength you have that can be applied toward realizing your dream?" You take the microphone confidently, and . . . write your response.

You replace the microphone at last and make your way through a wildly applauding audience to your waiting car. You sink into the luxurious upholstery and admire the car of your dreams for the few mintues it takes to drive to work.

Soon you arrive at your ideal place of work. Though you are busy, you take a moment to look around and cherish what you see and feel. Where are you? Are you inside or outside? How is the space defined? What are your furnishings like? What decorations do you see on the

walls? What sounds fill the air? Who else is there? How do they interact together?

Your work brings you many rewards now, since you began living
your dream. Remember the feelings you always wanted to have as you
worked? What are they? Choose from the list below, and add more of
your own:

creative	enthusiastic	serene	inspired
successful	strong	invigorated	acknowledged
important	cheerful	satisfied	independent
valuable	in the spotlight	respected	integrity
responsible	capable	organized	confident
appreciated	fascinated	excited	powerful

Imagine yourself gaining the rich recognition you deserve for your
contribution. What forms of acknowledgment do you receive for the
valuable work you do? Imagine the one person you most want to appreciate your value. Who is this person? What is it you want them to
know?

Now imagine you are back in your dream house. You settle back
into your dreaming chair again, feeling still more relaxed yet expectant. Your imaginary gaze comes to rest on your hand, which is holding your dream paycheck. Take a good look at this check. Who issued
it to you? What is the dollar amount? What work does it represent?
How will you distribute this money, ideally? Draw a picture of your
check, showing the details you envision. Then draw lines to divide it
into sections showing your ideal apportionment of the money as you
live your dream.

You realize you need to develop a new business card that
represents the special qualities your dream work has to offer. Picture
the design on your ultimate business card. What message does it convey about you? And about the value of what you have to offer? Examine the color, the artwork, the paper stock you will choose. Write some
words you might use. Now look closely at these words: each word you
decide to use will cost one thousand dollars, but you know it will be
well worth that price. What does your business card say? Draw a visual
representation of it.

Now, design a plaque to hang on the wall where you work. This plaque will display a very brief but powerful message. Everyone who sees it will instantly know what you're all about and will be enrolled to support you in living your dream. Write the message your plaque proclaims.

Beyond your work life, what feeling states do you most treasure? Do you value love, enthusiasm, thrills, comfort, pride, peace, suspense, laughter, romance, awe, fantasy, relaxation, spontaneity? Write at least thirty words to specify the feelings you want to fill your days with as you are living your dream.

Now, ask yourself which three words from your list are the most important to you. Use these words to form a statement that captures your dream—one that will energize and inspire you each time you read it. Write your statement now, in capital letters, in your Dream Book. Assign yourself the project of living for the entire current month with this statement as your top priority.

You stir in your easy chair, and realize that you have been imagining and writing so long, the sun has gone down and the first stars have come out to tease the darkness into laughter. Viewing the night sky with the same sense of wonder you had as a child, you declare your wish upon the first star, pausing to write it down. Alone but not lonely, you feel a deep sense of satisfaction with your own identity. Finally, you have found the ideal relationship you always longed for—not in the form of a friend or a lover—rather, it is the relationship you have *with yourself*.

Imagine getting up to put on some beautiful music. As the melody undulates through to your fingertips and the rhythm starts your toes to tapping, your body flows into a sparkling, carefree dance—fully feeling the *wholeness* of yourself. The holes and hunger that once yearned to be filled have blossomed into flowers and fruits.

It feels good to love yourself in this marvelous way. You are certain *you are* the person who can make you happy. The one who will love and honor you always, unconditionally, no matter what. The person who knows how wonderful you are, how beautiful you are inside. This person thinks only the highest thoughts about you, knowing that you are worthy of nothing less. This person knows all your dark corners and hidden secrets, and smiles tenderly and forgivingly at each lesson you have learned, even those that remain for you to learn.

Sitting down again, take a few moments to consider what you appreciate and like about yourself. What are your best qualities? What have you learned? Pretend you are another person who is preparing to introduce you as an honored guest at an intimate gathering of close friends. This person will sum up your most admirable qualities and character traits. Write a paragraph telling what will be said. Describe yourself in glowing terms, emphasizing the positive qualities which you consider most important.

Imagine loving yourself in the way you wish a lover would love you. Picture it: What would this lover do and say? Imagine loving yourself in these ways. You treat yourself as something special. You do special things for yourself, give yourself gifts. You anticipate your needs and provide for them, taking care of yourself with loving concern and affection. You love doing things to make you happy—not in a selfish way, but simply honoring yourself as an important and valuable being, worthy of the best you have to give. You have a new certainty that "My taking care of myself is best for others, too." You know that as you are well cared for, you are able to give generously out of your fullness, not reluctantly out of your emptiness. Pause to define the ways you now take loving care of your physical and mental well-being. Write these down.

Imagine walking over to a mirror. Look into it for a minute. You see many things; but focus on the dreamer. This dreamer—your best self—is beautiful, whole, complete, valuable, a person others love to be with. So alive. So vital and present. Look closely enough to see the star the world's been waiting for. Write a description of what you see.

See yourself choosing to create your dream, saying to yourself, "I made a decision, and I'm going to do it. The truth is, I'm the only one in the world whose destiny is to live *my* dream. I'm it. Others may or may not join me, but even if no one does, I know what I must do. From now on, it's not excuses, but *results*, for me." Write the action you will take today, based on this conviction.

Now your needs are richly met, your life is full and independent, and you choose to add another dimension. You feel naturally drawn to others who enhance and enrich your life. You move into a relationship with another special person who is equally whole, complete, and satisfied with his or her life. You and your dream partner in life come together to share each other's joys, successes, and difficult times. You openly inform each other: "I don't *need* you, I *want* to be with you, entirely out of free choice."

Your dream partner is as enthusiastic about his or her dream as you are about yours, and the fulcrum of your relationship is the sharing of your passion for life. Whenever you approach your partner, you read the invisible button he or she wears that says, "I'm living my dream: Ask me how!" Through constant updating on each other's dream status, you maintain your focus on success and movement, and on what needs to happen to bring about your dreams.

The emphasis of your communication together always begins with:

"This is what's making me happy; what's making you happy?"

"These are my accomplishments; what are your accomplishments?"

"This is what I think; what do you think?"

"This is what I feel; what do you feel?"

Thus, you lift your level of communication away from whatever isn't working, to what does work. You avoid bringing another problem to be resolved, another hurt to be atoned for, another apology required. You contribute meaningfully to the successful realization of each other's dreams.

Go to your imaginary drawing board now, and design an ad that will sell *you* to such an ideal partner. Your ad will capitalize on your best qualities—the true inner ones, not the superficial outward appearances. Capture the best you have to offer, and write your ad in a way that will appeal to a person with the qualities you desire to attract.

Now, see yourself in your dream leisure environment. This is your time for complete relaxation, rejuvenation, play and fun. What activities are available here? What is the scenery like? Who else is present? What sensations appeal to you? Are you active, working up a sweat, or quiet? Do you laugh hard and play hard, or do you smile contentedly and calmly amuse yourself? How much time do you want to spend here? How often do you want to come to this place? Imagine displaying photographs of yourself pursuing your favorite leisure activities in a place where you can remember the value of rest and relaxation in your life.

The exercise above is designed to stimulate you to visualize what living your dream would be like. Take all the time you need, to write at length about thoughts evoked by the questions in each area. Let your words stage a vivid scene of you living your dream. Let your life's innermost desires arise to your conscious attention, and form word-images on the paper before you. Really allow that inner dream to come forth fully, projected into every dimension of your experience. See yourself becoming your dream.

So, what *is* your dream? Ask yourself, "What do I want to accomplish in this lifetime? What do I want to be remembered for? What truly makes my heart sing? If I could do anything in the world I wanted, what would that be?" For now, set aside concerns about how impossible it might seem. Set aside the fear that if you actually said what you want, you would be miserable forever not being able to have it. If that fear rules you, you're already being miserable forever anyway—just not admitting it. And you won't have what you want until you know what it is!

ZEROING IN

When you decide to try a new dish, you have to know if you're going to make a cake, or spaghetti. You have to decide what you want. You have to find out what the ingredients are, and then you have to get them and set everything up so you can make it successfully. You can't put in all flour and no eggs, and you can't bake it in the bathroom. You have to prepare the right set of conditions for making a cake—otherwise, you might just turn up with spaghetti instead!

Let's do some more direct, open-eye investigations into your dream, to pin it down more.

First, consider some questions. What did you dream of being when you were young? What was it about that idea that was so appealing? What were the *experiences* you dreamed of having?

What trophy or award won as a child meant the most to you?

Why? What trophy or award would mean the most to you if you won it today? What would it mean, that you would value so much? Fame, success, applause, accomplishment—which is most important to you? What rewards do you find the most energizing?

Whom do you admire? What qualities in that person do you value—charisma, courage, stamina, integrity? In what ways does this person represent your ideal?

One of the most powerful tools for coming to understand who *you* really are, underneath all the "shoulds" and "buts" and external influences, is paying conscious attention to what you do and think. Read the list below, and for the next three days *notice* what is true for you:

NOTICE

- Notice what your first thought is on waking up.

- Notice, as you prepare for your day, whether you are excited about this day. Do you dread it? Is it "just another day"?

- Notice your thinking. Are you a positive or a negative thinker? Do you look for the good, or focus on the problem and whose fault it is?

- Notice what the most important part of your day is. The most enjoyable part?

- Notice what it is that you willingly set aside everything else to do.

- Notice whether money is a problem or a joy for you.

- Notice whether your day is organized in a way that will lead you to feel satisfied at its end.

- Notice the kinds of people you spend time with. Do you feel more alive around them? Or do you feel bored or drained?

- Notice whom you're attracted to, and for what reasons.

- Notice whom you try to impress.

- Notice your surroundings. Do they support you in being your best?

- Notice how you feel when someone asks you what work you do.

- Notice whether you are most interested in money, security or satisfaction. What do you work for?

- Notice whether spirituality is important to you. How much time do you give to it during the day? Do you live from a higher power? Do you put more energy into trusting, or doubting and worrying? Whom do you consider to be your authority?

- Notice how your body feels. Are you tense? Worn out? Energetic?

- Notice moments when you feel fully alive.

- Notice which activities move you to give nothing less than your best.

- Notice what you keep putting off.

- Notice where you passion lies. What creates real enthusiasm for you?

- Notice what you appreciate.

- Notice what you remembered; notice what you forgot.

- Notice who you put first.

- Notice who you put last.

- Notice what you pay attention to.

- Notice when you give your power away.

Notice if you notice, from one moment to the next. Do you pay attention to the feedback your feelings give you about what you are doing? What causes you to stop paying conscious attention?

One man said, "I realized from noticing the way I felt about work that I had been blind to how deadening my job is. It was something I hadn't wanted to see, but my body had been telling me all along. It was so hard to get up in the morning! I don't want to feel this way for twenty-five more years, so I know I have to make a change. I want to feel warm and human in my work, as I do when I'm reading bedtime stories to the kids."

Another woman reported, "I thought I had no choice but to deny my feelings. It's the modern way—tough, but a necessity. But leaving my two-year-old screaming, 'Mommy! Mommy!,' as I drove off every morning felt wrenching. I knew in my heart I belonged at home with her, for now. Once I began really letting myself feel what I feel, I saw clearly that it's more important for me to be with my child than anything else! I'll find a way to live more cheaply and make that possible."

Until you notice what's real, you're stuck with it, simmering below your level of awareness. Once you notice, the possibility of doing something about it becomes available to you. Use your Dream Book to write about insights that dawn on you as you practice the habit of *noticing* in your life. What have you noticed? What does it mean? What now? Just as you keep important legal and academic records, this personal account will provide you with a record of your developing awareness. Important insights often slip away in time, lost forever. Your self-awareness will be enhanced as you look back over your writing and understand the progression of your evolving self.

"I Would . . ."

Imagine you are looking back on your own life, nearing its end. Write your own list called "I would. . . ." Are the simplest joys and pleasures missing from your life as it is today? What changes need to be made, *before* it is too late? Write about this in your Dream Book.

The Time Is Now

If you suddenly found out you had only a brief time left to live, what would you do? Would you spend your time differently from the way you've lived the last month? Would your priorities change? What would become more or less important to you? What would you want to experience more of, or experience for the first time? Write your thoughts.

YOUR DREAM IN A NUTSHELL

Now it's time to go back and make sense of all the writing you've done so far. Your challenge is to develop a Dream Statement that captures the essence of the dream you will work on throughout the rest of this book, although your dream may evolve and change.

First, read everything you have written and highlight the most important ideas. Take notes, then build your words into one clear, simple statement that expresses your dream.

Here are some sample Dream Statements from students in my classes. They may assist you in pinpointing your dream.

My dream is to write a highly successful book and become financially independent.

My dream is to become a spiritual healer.

My dream is to let go of the past and be open to new growth.

My dream is to assist people in relieving pain and maximizing their potential through the impact of my documentary films.

My dream for now is to be the world's most wonderful parent and raise my children to be beautiful, loving people.

My dream is to travel all over the world as an actor, making people laugh.

Your dream will be different from any of those above. Whatever it is, it must come from the truth within you. It may have nothing to do with what your parents or anyone else expected you to be. Your own inner knowing is its only source.

STATE YOUR DREAM

Now, what *is* your dream? Once you have identified your Dream Statement, write it at the front of your Dream Book. Call and share it with your dream coach.

Dream Work Checklist

Before you go on, write answers to the following questions:

- What have you learned from noticing?

- How can you be more gentle with yourself?

- Are you living parts of your dream already? How do you feel about your life in relation to your dream now?

- What concrete steps toward realizing and living your dream have you already taken?

- What have you learned from your writing so far?

- What impact did the poem have on you? What are your thoughts about what you wrote? Would you like to write your own poem?

- How do you feel about living your dream so far?

- What is your dream? Say it over to yourself until it stays on the tip of your tongue. Your dream will soon seem like second nature to you.

When what you are about is bigger than day-to-day trivialities, you wake up every day with a purpose. Now that you know the goal, you are really ready to *begin*.

2

Clear Away Obstructions to Be
Clear about Your Dream

We are dominated by everything with
which our self becomes identified. We
can dominate, direct, and utilize everything from which we disidentify ourselves.

—Roberto Assagioli, *The Act of Will*

Iꜰ ʏᴏᴜ ᴡᴇʀᴇ inviting your best friend to come from far away and
stay with you for a month, you would need to clear out a room and
make space in your home. You might want to free up some time in
your schedule, also. Previously important items and activities would
be willingly set aside, as you excitedly prepared to welcome your
friend. Your friend's arrival might occupy a central place in your attention, as you formulated plans for your time together.

Your new dream requires adjustments in your old patterns in
much the same way. In order to make room for a new dream in your
life, the first step is to identify whatever interferes with your being able
to live the way you really want to. You probably have some bad habits,
like worry or self-condemnation, that get in the way. On top of that,
your spouse, your kids, the bills, the housework, a broken-down car,
might make your dream seem unachievable. You may also have some
beliefs that stop you. For example, your dream is to be a millionaire
philanthropist, but you've never met a millionaire who wasn't a power-
obsessed tyrant. With a belief like that lurking in your mind, how
could you become a millionaire yourself?

WHAT STANDS IN YOUR WAY?

Let's look more closely at the dream inhibitors in your life, those thoughts and habits that block your path to realizing your dream. Here are four sentence-completion exercises. For each, number a page in your Dream Book from 1 to 20, writing the specified sentence at the top. Read over this sample list, then, quickly and without pausing to evaluate your thoughts, write at least twenty different endings that apply to *you*.

MINDCLEANING—HABITS THAT SABOTAGE

A habit I allow to stand in the way of living my dream is:

1. Procrastinating.

2. Being disorganized.

3. Overcommitting myself.

4. Smoking cigarettes.

5. Staying up too late watching television.

6. Mindless eating.

7. Being obsessed about sugar.

8. Talking on the telephone too much.

9. Taking care of other people and not myself.

10. Allowing inertia to set in.

11. Not asserting myself.

12. Silent suffering.

13. Giving up too easily.

14. Being indecisive.

15. Being lazy.

16. Being irresponsible with money.

17. Not communicating when I don't like what someone says or does.

18. Taking on other people's problems and then resenting them.

19. Not preparing adequately.

20. Being overly perfectionistic.

Close your eyes and take a few minutes to consider your habits, and when you're ready, begin writing.

MINDCLEANING—BELIEFS THAT LIMIT

If you believe you can't possibly live your dream on your own, without someone else changing or helping you, you're probably not living your dream right now. If you reason that "No one in my family has ever been successful, so what chance do *I* have?" you probably aren't actively looking for every chance that might come along. If you see yourself as a failure, you probably aren't focusing on the possibility of being wildly successful. On the other hand, if you believe it is your destiny and your right to be tremendously successful, you have your eye set on that goal. I know a young man who believes he can do *anything* he wants, anywhere in the world—and he does. We all choose our beliefs, consciously or unconsciously, and then give them the power to allow or prevent our dreams.

What beliefs do you have that get in the way of living your dream? Number another page from 1 to 20, and make a list of beliefs that stand in your way. Here are some examples:

A belief I allow to stand in the way of living my dream is:

1. I'm not qualified; I don't know how; I'd have to have a college education.

2. It's too hard; I'd never have any fun if I worked as hard as my dream would require. I need to relax.

3. I have to wait until. . . .

4. Someone else should take care of me.

5. I don't have what I need to get started.

6. I don't have a sharp-enough mind or memory.

7. It's too late to start all over; I'm too old.

8. I have to wait for inspiration to strike.

9. I can't afford it.

10. Something or someone else has to come first, before my dream.

11. I'm terrified of making the needed changes; I might jeopardize my marriage/other relationship.

12. I don't deserve to be *that* happy.

13. I might fail; I probably couldn't succeed anyway.

14. I can't do it in *this* weather.

15. I'm waiting to be "discovered."

16. If I had too much, I'd feel guilty about others who don't have enough.

17. I need to take a nap (get a snack, make a phone call) first.

18. It's not what my parents want me to do.

19. I couldn't make as much money doing it.

20. Poor me—victim.

MINDCLEANING—RELATIONSHIPS

Not long ago I had made plans to attend a wedding reception, then I found my schedule closing in. My husband cheerfully offered to go alone and make an explanation for my absence, and I thankfully agreed: "Only if you tell the truth."

"What's the truth?" he asked.

"That I'm making last-minute revisions to my book, and I'm under a tight deadline," I said.

He came home reporting that people had responded with "oohs" and "aahs" and a great deal of curiosity that I was writing a book—my absence had taken on more significance than my presence probably would have. Making my dream a top priority with myself gave it increased validity in the world.

If family or outside obligations make your dream seem an impossibility, which particular people seem to be responsible for holding you back? Make a list of twenty *people* who "stand in your way," such as these examples:

A person I allow to stand in the way of living my dream is:

1. My father.

2. My mother.

3. My friend Sally.

4. My children.

5. My ex-spouse.

6. My wife.

7. My husband.

8. My boss Elsie.

9. My landlord.

10. My in-laws.

11. My imposing neighbor.

12. The loan officer at my bank.

13. The state licensing board.

14. My employees.

15. My sister.

16. My counselor.

17. My dogs.

18. My doctor.

19. The teacher who keeps giving me bad grades.

20. The mechanic who says my car needs expensive work.

Mindcleaning—Distractions

"It's too expensive." "I had a flat tire." "I'm too tired." Things often seem to become insurmountable obstacles that prevent people from living their dream. List the *things* that "stand in your way," like the following:

A thing I allow to stand in the way of living my dream is:

1. Housework.

2. Taxes.

3. Lack of money.

4. The government.

5. No computer/exercise machine/other equipment.

6. Lead feet.

7. My past.

8. Debt.

9. Not having the right clothes.

10. My weight.

11. Fear.

12. Bad luck.

13. Health problems.

14. The weather.

15. Television, watching my favorite shows.

16. The ball game.

17. My body isn't in good enough shape.

18. Lack of opportunity.

19. Unreceptive market.

20. Feeling tired and overwhelmed.

Congratulations! *You* are now the one who is in charge of what stops your dream. You have just reclaimed the power to *allow* things to stand in your way—or *not* to allow them! You can now choose. Read over your answers. What common threads or themes do you notice? What does this suggest to you? What new decisions will you make?

A NEW POINT OF VIEW

NEW HABITS THAT SUPPORT YOUR DREAM

Now go back and look at those four lists again, this time from a new point of view. Assume that you no longer choose to allow your habits, beliefs, other people, or things to stand in your way.

Next to each habit you listed, write a new habit you can use to replace the old dream-defeating one. Here are a few examples:

Old Habit	*New Habit*
Mindless eating	Conscious eating
Talking on the telephone too much	Turn answering machine on when I need to concentrate on working
Giving up too easily	Persistence and determination
Being indecisive	Staying focused
Being overly perfectionistic	Releasing and trusting

New Beliefs that Empower Your Dream

Write alternatives for each belief you listed. For example:

Old Belief	*New Belief*
It's too late.	Now's the best time I've got; it's never too late, and I'm excited about changing.
I'm not qualified.	My experience qualifies me; I will get any necessary qualifications.
I can't afford it.	I can't afford *not* to.
Poor me—victim.	Powerful me—creator.

Relationships that Energize You

For each name on your list of people, write: The change I am making in relation to this person is _____. For example:

1. The change I am making in relation to my father is that I will take the initiative and *act*, instead of just *reacting*. I will communicate to clear up misunderstandings, stop blaming, and take responsibility for needed changes.

2. The change I am making in relation to my mother is that I am owning my own life, and I will no longer allow myself to be manipulated by guilt.

3. The change I am making in relation to my friend Sally is that I am now able to say no. I choose how to spend my time wisely.

Focus vs. Distractions

Now examine each thing on your distractions list, and determine what can be done to overcome the obstacle to living your dream. You might be able to get around a lack of money by finding an affordable way to live your dream by taking initial small steps that lie within your present means; or by obtaining a loan. You might decide to erase the problem of debt by making a concentrated effort to pay off bills. If an unresolved issue from your past stands in the way of moving into the future, some counseling may be in order. Some items on the list, such as not having the right clothes or being overweight, or even having too much housework, could simply be crossed off or reprioritized, if you decide they are not valid reasons to prevent you from living your dream. Write a solution next to each item on your distractions list.

*   *   *

You now have an outline of what you can do to clear away to make room for your dream. Review this often, to remind yourself to continue making the changes you pinpointed. Note that more than anything else, the most important things to clear away are those old, self-limiting ideas that inhibit your growth and the full expression of your magnificence. By changing those ideas, you change your relation to the habits, beliefs, people and things you used to think were holding you back. When it comes right down to it, you and you alone hold the power to choose your life, by choosing the ideas on which your actions are based. Don't give that power away! Ultimately, there's only one answer to the question of what's standing in my way: *me, myself, and I.*

GIVE YOUR DREAM PRIORITY TIME

Clearing out your time schedule is a vital priority for living your dream. "Do you know how *busy* I am? I couldn't *possibly* take on one more activity!" This is an exclamation I often hear from active, involved individuals. Even when we're not spending our time exactly as *we* would prefer, we commonly feel that the demands pressed upon us preclude our having much of any choice in the matter. But if our dream is a last priority in our daily plan, it will also be the least likely outcome of our day, and our life.

If you go to a doctor or diet clinic for help in losing weight, you may be asked to keep a diary of your food intake. Only when you know what you are actually eating can you know what changes need to be made. The same is true of managing your time. It's important to begin keeping a record of how your time is spent. Once you have conducted a realistic assessment of the time available to you and the requirements made for your time, your options will be more apparent.

Become a Time Accountant

Begin by keeping a list of your activities during each of the seven days of one week. Write each activity in a column down the left side of a page, and write the days of the week across the top. Tally up the amount of time spent in each activity per day. Leave space for totals for the week on the right side. Your page might look something like the "Time Spent on Activities for a Week" chart (see page 37).

When you have filled out this chart for one week, study it carefully. Are you surprised at what it reveals? What do you observe about the way you spend your time? What changes can you make to manage your time optimally? Make a list.

In observing small children at play, I have noticed almost without exception their innate tendency to dump out the whole toy box before beginning to interact with the toys. They knock all the blocks down before beginning to build something new. Every piece of the Tinker Toy set must be pulled apart before a new construction is begun. Children inherently know the importance of starting anew, from the empty box or the blank table, when they want to create something new, all their own.

Create Your Ideal Day

Your time is your creative medium of expression, just like the child's box of toys. When you want to create a new set of priorities that highlights your dream, start like the small child with the blank table before you. Take a clean sheet of paper and write your Dream Statement across the top in large letters. Draw a chart where you can show activity time segments for an ideal day.

Decide which activities you want to accomplish each day. Begin by allocating set periods of time to work on your dream—periods that

Time Spent on Activities for a Week

ACTIVITY	NUMBER OF HOURS PER DAY							
	Mon	Tues	Wed	Thurs	Fri	Sat	Sun	Total
Sleep	7	8	6	7	6	9	8	51
Toilette	1	1	1.5	1	1	.5	1.5	7.5
Cooking	1.5	.5	2.5	2	.5	1.5	3	11.5
Eating								
Exercising								
Travel								
Work								
Telephone—work								
Telephone—social								
Interacting/spouse								
Quality time /children								
Entertainment								
Journaling								
Reading								
Television								
Dream Work								

are unlikely to be interrupted by other demands. Many people find that rising earlier in the morning serves this purpose. I know one man who had difficulty sleeping, and decided to work on his dream every time he woke up at 2:00 A.M.! He was able to turn a problem into an opportunity. Once you have set aside times for pursuing your dream, list your other activities in time segments, to represent the way you intend to spend your day. Combine optimal productivity with spaces for relaxation and rejuvenation. Plan a way to fit it all in. For an example, see the "Time Segments for an Ideal Day" chart below.

This single mother, whose dream is to be an interior designer, felt trapped by the many responsibilities of work and family. As she be-

Time Segments for an Ideal Day

MY ALL-NATURAL INTERIOR ENVIRONMENTS ARE IN HIGH DEMAND EVERYWHERE.

ACTIVITY	WHEN?
Work at the office and commute (arrange to go in at 7:00 A.M., so I can get off at 3:00)	
Interior design classes, three nights a week; homework three nights a week; rest and relax, one night a week	
Journal and reading	
Prepare and have dinner with the kids, catching up on their news and the events of their day	
Exercise and housework	
Morning preparations	
Sleep	

gins to plan an ideal schedule for herself, she writes her dream at the top of the list, and first fills in the hours her coursework and homework will require. She knows she will have to do some juggling and creatively manage her time, so she thinks of starting her workday early and combining tasks that can be handled simultaneously. Writing in her Dream Book, reading and keeping up an exercise routine are all important to her, so she schedules time for these activities, knowing that her success will depend on maintaining her personal well-being. Of course, she wants to assure that her children receive the attention they need from her, and her plan accommodates this also. She realizes she will have less leisure time, but already her mind is racing to figure new ways of saving minutes and consolidating tasks.

When you have drawn your chart and filled it in, experiment with it for a few days to see what adjustments are needed. The woman in the example above may realize she has forgotten to allow time for driving her son to his dance class one afternoon a week. She may then decide to have dinner out that day, or let her older child prepare the meal. Keep changing your chart until you have a plan that works.

Note that this approach is opposite to the one we typically use in our everyday lives. Cognizant of the day's requirements, we begin tackling one job after another, often in whatever order the most pressing problems appear. We hope eventually to get around to those inner priorities that we keep a secret, often even from ourselves—but somehow the day fills up with so many other things. Or, perhaps our personal style is to do what we feel like doing first, leaving our obligations to be dealt with later. Our dream boils away on the back burner and is never handled in a responsible manner on a day-to-day basis. The planned approach, on the other hand, emphasizes putting first things—your dream—first.

Schedule Your Dream

Once you have completed the preceding two charts, you are ready to take charge of your time, and the following method is the most effective one I know for doing so. Begin by creating a weekly chart with a key activities list to fit your individual lifestyle. See the sample key list below the following chart (page 40). What categories

SCHEDULING MY DREAM							
HOUR OF DAY	Mon	Tues	Wed	Thurs	Fri	Sat	Sun
5:00–6:00 A.M.							
6:00–7:00							
7:00–8:00							
8:00–9:00							
9:00–10:00							
10:00–11:00							
11:00–12:00							
12:00–1:00 P.M.							
1:00–2:00							
2:00–3:00							
3:00–4:00							
4:00–5:00							
5:00–6:00							
6:00–7:00							
7:00–8:00							
8:00–9:00							
9:00–10:00							
10:00–11:00							
11:00–12:00							
12:00–1:00 A.M.							
1:00–2:00							
2:00–3:00							
3:00–4:00							
4:00–5:00							

KEY:

Dark blue	=	sleep
Yellow	=	morning preparations
Green	=	reading
Gold	=	living my dream and taking steps toward it
Rose	=	journaling
Gray	=	time at office
Pink	=	time on phone at home
Black	=	doing nothing—wasted time
Light blue	=	watching television
Orange	=	eating
Red	=	playing
Yellow-green	=	driving, errands
Purple	=	housework

will you need to add? Which ones do not apply to you? Make any needed substitutions. Then make copies of your blank chart, to use over the next four weeks.

You can use a set of colored pencils to color in each block of time according to the key that categorizes how the hours are spent. Use this chart each day to monitor your use of time. This requires careful attentiveness to the clock and what you are doing. But it has been known to bring about powerful revelations to those who took the trouble to do it. What do you observe about your use of your time? Write your observations in your Dream Book, listing any recommendations for modifying your future use of time.

Recently, I noticed I was becoming increasingly exasperated at my own seeming lack of time to do the things I wanted to do. Having taught the systematic inventory of time allocation for several years, I decided once again to begin using it myself. I was doing a job that required many phone calls and the management of complicated arrangements. I was being paid to do it, so why was I feeling so frustrated? I was not too astonished to learn that the job was taking far more time than I had thought.

"If I focused that much time on things I love and things I want to bring into reality," I reasoned, "I would be loving each day and bringing those things into reality." With this information in hand, I immediately made a choice—to give notice and resign from the position.

Others have also received valuable insights:

I can see that quality time with my husband is almost nonexistent.

I am faced with the reality that a large part of my time is spent doing favors for friends and relatives—things I didn't really want to be involved in at all. But I rationalized that they wouldn't take *that* much time!

I was just sitting down to watch television when I realized, "How can I let myself get away with watching television for six hours, when I say I want to be a famous writer?"

I realized how little time I'm actually putting into living my dream.

There's no time for play and fun here! No wonder I'm beginning to feel burned out.

I became much more conscious about the choices I make that affect the way my time is distributed.

Part of my dream is to be an excellent parent. Before, I had felt a little resentful of all the time I spent helping the kids with their homework, cooking good meals, even going for counseling. But when I began to categorize these activities as part of my dream, I realized how much fulfillment they offer. It brings me great pleasure to be succeeding at what I have declared I want.

I found out I fool myself about my "work efficiency."

I've been neglecting to set aside any time for *myself*!

People often discover they could take more responsibility to manage their time efficiently. Designing your dream schedule can put you back in the driver's seat of your own day. Whenever I find myself doing something I don't like, I stop to ask myself, "Is this part of living my dream?" If not, I begin working to change it. I may stop doing it, figure out another way of getting it done, or make it part of living my dream. If it is something that has to be done to prepare for living my dream, I am happier knowing that I am on track.

If you are serious about living your dream, rearranging your time may be a necessity. Is your dream any less important than those of other great leaders who use every resource available to accomplish what they envision?

How do you feel about your use of your time? Is most of your time spent doing what is most important to you? Are you beginning your day by writing a statement about what you intend to accomplish? Are you ending your day by following up on it, noting which of your intentions were actually accomplished, and congratulating yourself on them? Does your time chart match your dream? Is your allocation of your time consistent with your commitment to living your dream? Define any changes you intend to make, keeping in mind the old adage, "You love the life you live, when you live the life you love."

PUT YOUR DREAM INTO PICTURES

When you choose to have something new in your life—a new wardrobe, car, house—it takes time, energy and work to get it. Time and energy are needed to find the items you want and buy them. It takes even more work to keep things in good condition for continued use and beauty.

It is the same with a dream. In order to have your dream *work*, you will need to do some dream work.

Now that you have cleared away many of the obstacles to living your dream, the most important thing you can do next is to become very clear about what your dream will look like. It is time to create a Dream Board—a symbolic visual representation of your dream.

CREATE A DREAM BOARD

When I was teaching school, my students loved the assignment to create a collage of pictures of all the things that represented who they were, "a collage about *me*." One blonde fifth-grader cut out pictures with powder-soft colors, ribbons, ruffles and lace. When she held her creation up to show, she exclaimed, "Yeah! That's who I am!" It strengthened her pride in her own femininity. Once the students identified in their minds *who* they were, a focus and sense of purpose came. They stepped more surely. Their self-esteem came from within, no longer dependent upon comparisons with anyone else.

The idea was so valuable with these students that I adapted it as an inspirational aid for adults who wanted to live their dreams. Dream Boards soon became a vital part of the "Live Your Dream" process. This is an extremely valuable project. As it takes form, you will begin to treasure the ideas you are creating, and the picture can be worth a thousand words! Your Dream Board will take you one step further, beyond who you are now to what you could become.

Look through magazines and cut out pictures and words that portray your dream. If you have artistic talent, you may prefer to do your own drawings and designs. Arrange these on a piece of poster board to create an attractive picture of the *you* you want to be. Include pictures or photographs of the aspects of your life—your ideal body, family, friends, relationship, home, car, work, accomplishments, finances, leisure activities, vacations—anything and everything that's important to you.

All around us, ads and commercials lure us to identify ourselves with slender, sexy bodies leaning against newly purchased sports cars, reclining in fantasy dream homes, and lounging with adoring partners on luxury ocean liners or pristine tropical beaches. Commercial advertising is predicated on the powerful effectiveness of such images to get us to bring these desirable experiences into our lives. In creating your Dream Board, you are designing your own ad and picturing your own perfect life. Be as creative as you like, but follow one rule: you can only paste in a picture when you are willing to take the action required to make it a reality. Be sure that the images you select belong to *you*—don't borrow ideas from someone whose values differ from yours.

All kinds of materials may be used imaginatively in this project. Participants in my classes have even created mobiles, or used photo cubes or their bathroom mirrors, as background surfaces for their Dream Boards. Many popular phrases from advertising can be adapted to serve your purposes. One person used an ad for dog food: "It's time for Fit & Trim." Another chose the army slogan, "Be all that you can be." Yet another added, "The sky's the limit," but someone else in the class responded, "That's *too* limiting for me!"

A woman named Anna reported that she had started to attach a photo of a "picture-perfect model house." Then she stopped. "That's something *other* people want," she realized. "It's not important to *me*. I like the house I have."

Joel, a maintenance engineer, said, "I come from a pretty limited background—negative, inhibited. If I were to show this Dream Board to anyone I grew up with, they'd probably say, 'Well, who do you think *you* are, anyway?' But this gives me the first glimpse I've ever really had of what I could become! And every time I look at it, I think, 'Sure! Why not me, too! I can do that!'"

Joan, a successful businesswoman, said, "Two weeks ago, I made a Dream Board with an ideal house that was light and airy, and a beautiful pool surrounded by greenery. Today, I signed the papers on that house!"

When you finish your Dream Board, display it in a prominent place where it can remind you often and reinforce where you're headed. You have now declared your dream. And when you declare, life supports you, and conditions around you begin moving into place to make your dream a reality. The movement may be subtle at first, but watch for each little sign of it. *Record these* in your Dream Book as documentation of building momentum.

Talk to Yourself

In addition, begin having conversations with yourself in the mirror. Imagine your dream as a reality, and talk to yourself about it. If it feels silly to do this, note that part of what you are working through is the sense of separation between where you are now and where you see yourself in your dream. Practice this daily as you are brushing your teeth and combing your hair.

Use All the Coaching You Can Get!

Call your dream coach every day. Read your Dream Statement and a summary of your day's accomplishments. Reinforce each other for the steps you're taking in doing your dream work.

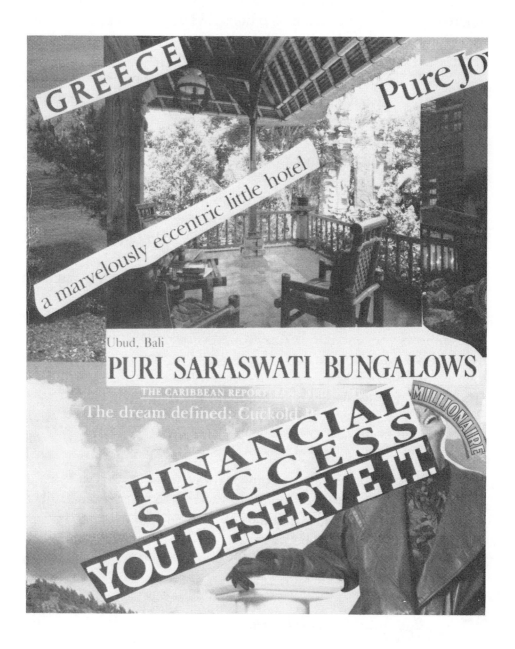

Sample Dream Board
Words and Pictures #1

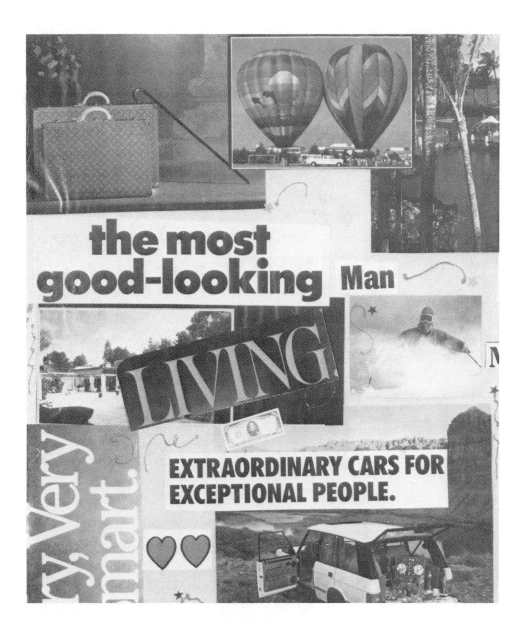

Sample Dream Board
Words and Pictures #2

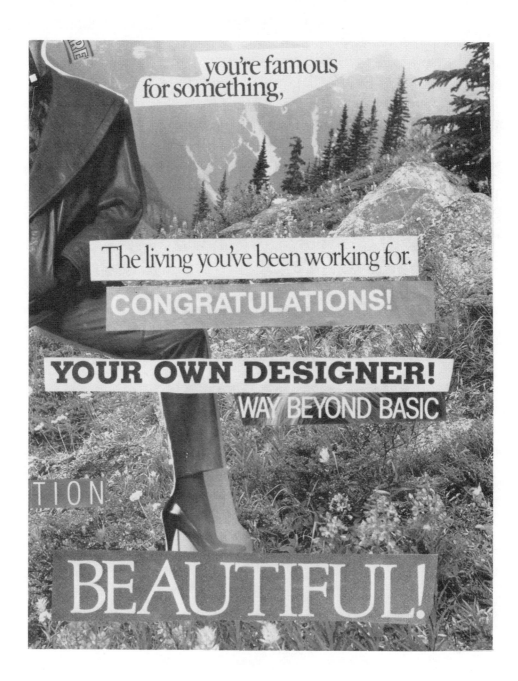

Sample Dream Board
Words and Pictures #3

You've made an important start. Are you planning your schedule? Stay with it! Acknowledge yourself for your successes. You're doing great!

Dream Work Checklist

- *Visualize* your dream.

- Write answers in your Dream Book to these questions:

    What are you learning by visualizing each morning?

    How do you go about it?

    Are there difficulties or resistances to overcome?

- Schedule and review your goals (dream steps) and progress each day.

- Complete all the writing exercises in Chapter 2 and chart how you spend your time.

- Write a summary of what you learned by charting your time.

- Make a Dream Board and display it prominently.

- Hold conversations with your mirror image every morning.

- Read helpful books.

- Call your coach each day and ask:

    What did you do today to live your dream?

    What did you *notice* and learn from noticing?

    What actions have you taken today about your dream?

    Repeat and register for your partner what you heard. Use phrases like, "I heard. . . ." "I'm not sure. . . ." "Did you say . . . ?" Confront your partner lovingly when necessary. Write in your Dream Book about insights you receive.

3

A Winning Attitude

> Within each of us lies the power of our
> consent to health and to sickness, to
> riches and to poverty, to freedom and to
> slavery. It is we who control these, and
> not another.
>
> —Richard Bach, *Illusions*

HAVE YOU EVER found yourself in situations where you look around and wonder, "How did I ever get here?" The simple truth is that we participate, either knowingly or unknowingly, in the process of getting where we are. The more we observe that and pay attention, the more aware we become.

At times we all want to say, "Who, *me*? I had nothing to do with creating this mess! It just happened!" Or, "It was so-and-so's fault—there's nothing *I* could have done!" We feel absolutely powerless over the situation—like helpless victims. The last thing we want to hear when we're all caught up in our "victim story" is anything about being accountable and responsible!

Yet, it is assuming accountability that gives us power over our lives. The more we practice the habit of acting from a position of responsibility, the more effective we become as human beings, and the more successful we become as managers of our lives.

BE ACCOUNTABLE

So let's assume, just for the moment, that you are able to see yourself as responsible and accountable. This doesn't mean, of course, that you're in control of anyone else's experience. But for your own experience, no matter what the situation, let's assume that you take responsibility (*not blame, not fault, but responsibility!*). Now let's try a switch in perspective. For example, instead of saying, "You really hurt my feelings when you criticized me like that," I could say, "I chose to let your criticism hurt me. I allowed you to be in charge of *my* feelings for a moment. I recognize your right to your opinions— I can either agree and learn from your criticism, or appreciate that your view may differ from mine. It's interesting that once again I notice that I've put someone else in charge of *my* feelings. I see what I can learn from this!"

Write Your Victim Story—and Turn it Around

Now, do some work in your Dream Book. Draw a line down the center of a page, and write a title for the left-hand column: Victim Story; and for the right-hand column: Re-told from Accountability. Think of a situation in which you felt like a victim. Write the story briefly, emphasizing how helpless you felt. Then use the adjacent space on the right to rewrite the event from the opposite point of view, emphasizing how your experience was caused, directly or indirectly, by various things you did. Explore thoroughly how your action (or inaction) contributed to the outcome of the situation. Do this for as many situations as you can, in which you felt powerless in the hands of some other person or circumstance.

Victim Story	*Re-told from Accountability*
I had just replaced the tape deck in this van. I parked in the lot outside where I work, in broad daylight. Someone broke in and stole it again!	Actually, I did know about the rash of burglaries in that lot lately. We were advised to use the protected lot across the street—but I was late for work, so I decided to take a

Can't you trust *anyone* these days? It makes me just sick!

chance. It's a hard lesson for me about learning to get up earlier. Maybe I'll buy some insurance now, too.

That husband of mine! He's got to go and buy whatever he wants, *now*! We haven't been able to save anything for the future. I'm at my wit's end!

Well, if the truth be known, the things we've bought had their appeal for me, too. I could have put my foot down and just said "no." Perhaps I could work with him to develop a plan for saving.

Those earaches I had when I was little—they were so painful! I would lie in my bed, crying and crying, but no one came to see what was the matter. My parents never really cared. I was so alone whenever I hurt!

Did I ever think of going to ask for help? Gosh, I think I was determined to keep my pain a secret— just so I could feel sorry for myself, or what? My parents probably had no idea. Even today I hesitate to ask for help. I need to work on this some more.

Now, go ahead and write your victim stories in your Dream Book. You may find it valuable to repeat this exercise whenever you catch yourself feeling victimized, until there's no more victim left in you. When you're finished, go on to the next exercise.

THE CHILD AS PURE, UNRESTRICTED ENERGY

Sometimes, before we can get up and move on, we must first examine where we are. So now do a little daydreaming. You may choose either to read the following section through first and then settle into your reverie, or to make a tape recording of it (read very slowly) to guide you through the sequence of imaginings. When you're ready, get comfortable, close your eyes, and allow yourself to drift back in time.

Visualize: The Child in You

Imagine yourself as a very small child, full of love, joy, playfulness, spontaneity, energy, laughter, fun. You are without a care in the world, and you are so irresistibly cute! You skip down the street, arms flying, hair blowing in the breeze, singing at the top of your voice. The world is your playground, put there expressly for your amusement, and you lavishly exercise dominion over all you see. You instruct the flowers to grow and the houses to line up in a row. You laugh with abandon, you scream when frightened and you cry with unrestrained shrieks when you're hurt. Look carefully, to observe this charming little child. What are you wearing? Where are you playing? What are the toys you treasure? What does your mother scold you for doing too wildly?

This little child is a shining star, and it has never occurred to the child to question it. You sparkle before an audience, and you adore attracting all the attention and admiration you can command. You perform with utter abandonment—see yourself, there? What is your favorite act to play? Look at your audience—a grandparent or uncle, perhaps, or friends of the family. What response does your performance elicit from them? Do you make them laugh or clap or praise you? Or do you go for shock value, sly snickering and feigned horror or fear? How powerful you feel, to have such a strong impact on all those big people!

You love to pretend. Pretending is magical—it can make you anything you want to be. Experience this child-self. What does this child love pretending to be? Are you the beautiful fairy princess or invincible Superman? Are you the masked bandit; king of the mountain; the wicked witch; a lion tamer; a pirate on the high seas; a mysterious wandering gypsy; a flying trapeze artist; Merlin the magician; a race car driver; a comical clown; an adventurous explorer of outer space?

Which side do you want to be on—cops or robbers; the good guys or the bad guys; the peasants or the royalty; the caretaker, or the organizer? Imagine you are there right now, playing the games you used to play. How do you feel? What costumes do you put on? What part do you play with other kids? What are your most pleasurable roles, and what is it about the experience that you relish so much? Recall a time when you felt:

- Powerful.

- Loving.

- Playful.

- Fully self-expressive.

- Productive.

- Fully nourished.

- Passionately alive.

- Responsible and important.

- Joyful.

What did each of these experiences mean to you? What conclusions did you draw from it at the time? Live with these questions for a few days. Sleep on them, and record your insights upon awakening.

The marvelous experiences you treasured as a child are still a part of you. But you may discover in them certain aspects of yourself that you put aside long ago, to become a "grown-up." Perhaps you overheard someone saying, "Oh, don't pay any attention to him/her; he/she's *crazy!*" and from then on you imprisoned that joyful, spontaneous, uninhibited part of yourself. Perhaps you encountered someone who had rigidly denied the feelings you were freely expressing. When this person reacted to you with shock and dismay, you concluded it was unacceptable to be that way. Can you recall the first time you decided it was not okay to be who you are? What happened that made you decide you could no longer be that way?

Now, consider further: do you really need to maintain that decision to shut down your aliveness? What would happen if you dared to be the real you today? Which experiences and which qualities would you choose to reclaim?

These hidden resources within you—the parts of your aliveness that have been suppressed—are the atomic energy of your being. Splitting the atom of suppression will release the boundless power of your being. You will reconnect your outer reality with the inner driving force that impels you to express your best. You will operate from the conviction of being who you *must*, and that conviction will be the ballast that steadies you through the stormy challenges life blows your way.

What if you went around being spontaneous, joyful, loving, powerful and expressive all the time? Would you be dangerous, or a happy, fulfilled, warm individual? How would you act if you *knew* you had nothing to lose? How outrageous would you be? Or, restated: How *will* you act, knowing you really do have nothing to lose? How outrageous *will* you be?

John was a serious, reserved, extremely intellectual man whose hesitancy to make a decision or take action until he considered every piece of information had prevented him from taking advantage of several important opportunities in his career. John began awakening the childlike energies pent up inside him through the use of puppets. "Gladly" was the puppet personality who was unreservedly *glad* to have finally emerged. Gladly went around noticing everything as if for the first time, taking delight in flowers and freckles and frowns. There was nothing analytical or logical in Gladly—he responded instantly, and always from the point of view of the delighted participant. Everybody liked Gladly.

Gladly had a tiny mitten puppet he wore on *his* hand, named Frankly. Frankly was playful, ready to fire off a spontaneous answer to any question without pausing to think. Frankly could be counted on to tell the truth as he saw it. He made everyone laugh.

When John entertained audiences with his puppets, dimensions of his personality were revealed that no one had ever suspected were there. He was lively, quick, funny and intuitive. Gradually, through projecting his childlike energies into the puppet personalities, John began to integrate these qualities into his everyday life. He no longer felt rigid and constrained, and his sense of adventure soon overcame his former hesitancy. John came to feel so good about himself that he began seeking Frankly's ready advice on major decisions. More and more, he chose the "Gladly" and "Frankly" aspects of expression over his old compulsiveness. Whenever he did this, his life became more fun. People enjoyed his company, and finally he changed his career to pursue an artistic endeavor, something he had always wanted to do.

Freeing up your child-self is a choice that is available to you, too. So let yourself go exploring into your own hidden dimensions. You may discover a vein of gold there, waiting to be mined. Stop now, and do some writing in your Dream Book about the questions this section has posed. When you finish, write a single sentence that summarizes your insights.

NO MORE UNFINISHED BUSINESS

In the last chapter, you began to work on clearing out old beliefs that were in the way. Now, to continue the clearing out and making new space for your dream, turn your attention to things in your life that are incomplete. If you haven't balanced your checkbook in three months, or your garage is stacked with clutter from floor to ceiling, you may be unaware that your mental energy is tied up in those things. You simply put them out of your mind, and they don't bother you—although one of these days you do plan to do something about them.

The fact of the matter is, every situation left hanging subconsciously reduces the reserves of your mental energy. We often don't realize this until we clear out and handle the mess. Then, how light and free we feel!

This phase of "Live Your Dream" was critical to the life changes a woman named Sara decided to make. Here is her story:

> I started in my garage, going through boxes and boxes of stuff. I would take everything out, consider where I could put it, and end up cramming it all back into the box. How do you unpack a box of stuff you don't even want? There were my ex-husband's trophies; after carrying them with me through four moves, I finally realized he must not want them!
>
> But what really hit me was looking through my house. I had

accumulated generations of family heirlooms and hundreds of valuable antiques. All these things needed a home! I realized I had
designed my life around having a place for all this stuff. It was not
part of my dream. But I had made it a part of my reality.

What I really want, after all these years of respectable responsibility, is to be a free spirit. Now that I can do whatever I like,
I want to be a gypsy! I want to pick up and go on impulse to new
places. I want to travel all over the world, without a schedule or
a return reservation home.

I knew I had to let the stuff go. You can't be a gypsy with an
antique hutch. It just won't fit into a backpack!

Sara proceeded to invite the class to a garage sale to end all garage
sales. She sold everything she had, and set off to seek her fortune.
Now I never know where her next phone call will come from, because
Sara is happily living her dream all over the world.

Your clearing out may not be quite so comprehensive as Sara's,
but your results, like hers, are sure to move you closer to living your
dream. As you eliminate excess possessions, take care to remain true
to yourself. If you love your old, threadbare bathrobe, you may choose
to keep it and get rid of that new one you never really cared for. Just
keep your focus on identifying whatever stands in the way of living
your dream—that's what needs to go.

CLEANING CENTERS

So, here's an exercise to free all that powerful creative energy.
Imagine you are dividing your life into the following areas: work, lei-
sure, physical body, home, relationships, finances, self-development.
Write these categories, spread around a blank page in your Dream
Book. Circle each, like this:

Major Areas of My Life

(Work)   (Leisure)

(Self-Development)

(Physical Body)   (Home)

(Relationships)   (Finances)

What would happen if you made an all-out spring-cleaning effort on your life? To enable you to clean out your life, clear up any leftover business and launch your dream with fresh energy. Begin by looking at each area you have circled in your Dream Book.

You have created the beginning of a cluster diagram. Each circle represents a major category that encompasses related areas. Look at each circle, and add subcategories to create a more complete picture of your life. Draw other circles branching out from each main category:

Details of Each Area of My Life

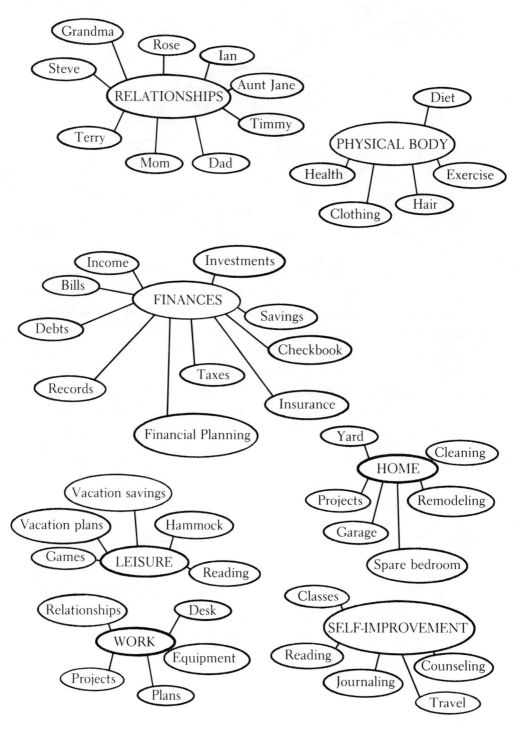

Continue expanding your diagram until each area of your life is represented.

Next, use the cluster diagram to create a list of all the things that need to be done, to free you to live your dream. For each item on your diagram, close your eyes and ask yourself, "What feels incomplete in this area? What have I been intending to get done? What have I been putting off?" In your Dream Book, write a To-Do list for each of the seven major categories in your cluster diagram.

THINGS TO COMPLETE

Be thorough and unflinching, now. Your lists may seem impossible to accomplish at first, but avoid the temptation to turn back, quit, or omit difficult items. Just pause to write candidly in your Dream Book about what you are learning from your lists. Are you willing to complete things?

Here are some additional questions to guide you for each category. Use them to scrutinize each area of your life. Add to your To-Do lists whatever suggestions these questions bring to mind.

PHYSICAL BODY: WHAT NEEDS COMPLETING?

Stand in front of a mirror and examine your body. What actions do you want to take to make your body a reliable vehicle to support your dream plans? How is your hairstyle? Is your general appearance appropriate for someone who is living your dream? Need to lose a few pounds? What concrete actions will you take? When did you last have a physical exam? Have you been putting off dental work or medical treatment? How about an eye exam—need new glasses? What skin care products or treatments are in order? How is your hearing?

Oh, yes, and about that exercise routine. What is your plan? How will you implement it and reward yourself when you carry through?

Are cigarettes or drinking a problem? How about joining a clinic or support group? Are there drugs you want to eliminate? Is it time to kick the sugar habit? How will you improve your diet? Specify concrete steps to take.

Now, for the wardrobe. As you look in your closet and dresser drawers, what pleases you? What negative reactions do you have? Are you still saving clothes from a decade ago "just in case" those styles come back again? Would someone who is zooming into the future, living their dream, be hanging on to such relics of the past? Isn't it time to clean out all your closets and drawers? Plan to throw or give away anything you no longer wear.

And what about mending, shoe repairs, laundry, dry cleaning? Add specific tasks to your To-Do list. What items need to be purchased to complete or enhance your wardrobe? Would someone representing your dream need fashionable clothing, new shoes, respectable underwear, in order to feel their best? Coats and umbrellas are items you'll want to have ready and waiting, when you're heading out the door to live your dream.

Home: What Needs Completing?

Go through each room of your house and throw away or give away anything that is no longer used. What repairs are needed? What appliances need to be fixed or replaced? What maintenance work should be done? What remodeling projects are pending or necessary? Look around for borrowed items and return them, and retrieve items you have loaned out and now want back. Cancel subscriptions to magazines you never have time to read, and get rid of all those musty stacks of back issues you feel so guilty about neglecting.

What about the exterior of the house, yard and garden? Do windows, doors and locks need repair or replacement? Is it time to repaint? Do trees and bushes need trimming? Have you been meaning to plant some fruit trees or flowers? What other yard work would you recommend, if you were creating your ideal surroundings? Do it!

While you're outside, have a look at your car(s)! How does yours look? Is it clean? Do the trunk and glove compartment need straightening out? Is it due for waxing or new tires? What about routine service and maintenance? Do you have a regular service schedule, or do you need to make one? Are there repairs you've been putting off? What will it take to restore your car to perfect order? Should you be making arrangements to purchase a car?

WORK: WHAT NEEDS COMPLETING?

What tasks at work have been left unhandled? Is your work schedule manageable? Is your office a mess? Do certain jobs seem to wait stacked up on your desk forever? When was the last time you cleaned out your files? How orderly is your desk?

What changes can you make at work, to create an ideal place where you can live your dream? Have you been intending to ask for a raise? Are your travel and expense reimbursement forms up-to-date? What about other records you are responsible for keeping? What meetings need to be scheduled? What equipment needs repair? What improvements would you recommend?

What have you been wanting to communicate to your employer, your employees or your co-workers? Any letters that could be written? Make a plan to do these things now.

RELATIONSHIPS: WHAT NEEDS COMPLETING?

Consider each person on your cluster diagram. What truths have been left uncommunicated? What messages need to be delivered? What regrets, resentments, hurts, criticisms and apologies have been withheld? What stands between you and this person? What prevents you from being completely open and honest with him or her? What keeps the two of you from meeting each other's eyes unguardedly?

What lies, half-truths and withheld truths need to be cleaned up? What broken promises and agreements need to be acknowledged and resolved, either by keeping them or by making a new agreement?

What can you do to repair or resolve any damaged relationships? Do you need to forgive someone? What amends do you want to make, if your actions have hurt or damaged someone else? Is there a relationship that has died or become injurious and needs to be ended?

What acknowledgments do you want to give to people who have made special contributions to your life? Make a list of letters you will write, phone calls you will make, and talks you will have in person.

Finances: What Needs Completing?

Let's start with the basics. Is your current income enough, or do you need to find a way to increase it? What will you do? Is your checkbook balanced? Is your money being handled the way it will need to be handled when you are living your dream? There'll be no time for interruptions from creditors then, and worrying about how to make ends meet. Better get in practice right away: plan a budget and stick to it. Pay all your bills. Contact everyone you owe money to, and make arrangements you can keep, to pay them. Also, collect any money that is owed to you or your company.

Are your tax records current? Do you owe any taxes? Do you need some help figuring or managing your taxes? Are your tax files organized and accessible? What else needs to be done to organize your financial records and bring them up to date?

And what about security for the future? Perhaps a money management class would be timely? When did you last review the coverage and rates on each of your insurance policies—health, auto, life, homeowner's? Is an updating in order? Have members of your household been informed about these policies and where they are kept? What about retirement and personal investment plans? What actions do you need to take to prepare for later years?

Self-development: What Needs Completing?

What are the ways you'd like to be improving yourself? Have you known for a long time that you might benefit from some personal counseling? Now is the time to schedule it! Have you considered using a personal image consultant or having a make-up makeover? What about video feedback on your personal presentation? What personal growth seminars do you want to take?

Are there educational classes you would like to take? How about going back to school for a degree? And remember those other areas you always wanted to learn more about, and skills you'd like to perfect. A class in swimming, guitar, tennis, drama, speech, cooking, religious instruction, etc., might broaden your horizons.

What are the books you've been wanting to read? Have you made a list of them, and gotten started yet? Plan a reading schedule. What about audio and videotapes you want to buy?

Leisure: What Needs Completing?

Are you making adequate time for leisure activities? What enjoyable ways of relaxing have you been putting off? What games or equipment do you want to purchase? What vacation plans do you want to arrange? What changes can you make in your home and schedule to enable you to enjoy your leisure time more?

What kind of recreation do you want more of? What people and places would you like to visit? What friends and family members would you enjoy spending more time with? What kind of fun do you wish you had more of? What makes you laugh? What activities do you put off until vacation or retirement time, when you could be enjoying them now?

With the busy schedule needed to live your dream, planning time for relaxation and fun is essential to counterbalance the work.

That's a lot to think about, and it may be a lot to do. Your completion list may seem formidable at first. You'll need to approach it one item at a time. When you finish your To-Do lists, go over them and project a date by which you will complete each item, writing the date in the margin. Then throughout the next weeks, work on completing all the items. The more you do, the better you'll feel!

If there is something you are unable to complete immediately, figure out how long it will take before you can do it, and mark this date on your calendar. For example, if you need to have a new roof put on your house but you can't afford to do it just yet, determine how long it will take to save the money, make a plan for setting a certain amount aside regularly and write your targeted completion date on your calendar. This will clear your mind.

Once you have completed long-term unfinished business, you will find that monthly maintenance is much simpler. Your life, like an automobile, will work best when you stick to a routine maintenance schedule. So get in the habit of handling and completing each task and each communication *right on the spot*. Then review and update your completion list regularly at the beginning of each month when you sit down to pay your bills.

As a participant in one of my classes said, "Handling completions is like putting the tail on the kite—you're getting your dream ready to fly." People have achieved impressive results through handling needed completions:

I found things I thought I'd lost.

I made plenty of space to organize my stuff.

I have the things I need at my fingertips.

I freed my attention to focus on what I really want to do.

I stopped berating myself for all the things I *hadn't* done.

I let go of excess baggage I'd been dragging around.

I was healed of some painful emotions I had buried.

I restored my faith in myself. I am confident I can handle new things.

I have a ton of energy—more than I ever thought possible!

I feel free and in charge.

I laugh more.

A student named Beca achieved remarkable results through clearing out and completing things. Confronting the aspects of her life that were inconsistent with her dream was frightening to her, because it meant eliminating much of what she had grown comfortable with. Having been a successful financial planner and seminar leader for years, Beca had established herself in a predictable and orderly lifestyle. The only missing ingredient was the *life.*

When Beca examined where her real energy and enthusiasm lay, she found it in her love for dance and choreography! She finally understood why she was unable to tolerate music playing in her house— she *had* to deny that part of herself to remain a financial planner. Beca left her job, her old house and many former relationships behind, to start out anew. Now, her teenage daughters complain that *she* is playing the music too loud. Beca is committed one hundred percent to making a new career for herself in the field she loves—a choice made possible only by being willing to let go and clear out her attachments to a past that no longer suited her.

GIVE YOURSELF CREDIT

As you work on completing things, make a point of writing in your Dream Book what you have accomplished and how it supports you in living your dream. Acknowledge yourself warmly. Put up a large piece of poster board, and use it to brag about your completions. Tell them to someone who can be counted on to acknowledge you. Give yourself credit often for how good you feel about each burden lifted from your back. Have a party, and ask people to bring a list of things they have completed, for the purpose of acknowledging and celebrating everyone's completions. Set up a system to ensure that you receive the rewards you deserve, so your motivation to complete things will be constantly renewed.

Each month, write an entry in your Dream Book beginning, "By cleaning out and handling things, I. . . . " Your energy will be freed for greater and greater pursuits, once your focus is no longer diffused in so many directions.

A POSITIVE ATTITUDE SETS YOU UP TO SUCCEED

When I was little, I was given a special gift by my mother. Every morning, she would come into my room and greet me with a hug and a cheerful, "Wake up! It's a beautiful day!" Some mornings, she would modify that to, "Wake up! It's a beautiful *rainy* day." She was teaching me to live my life anticipating and finding the beauty in every day—sunny or rainy. I grew up expecting my days to be beautiful. My mother's attitude spread joy all around her.

More than anything else, our attitude in approaching a task will determine our success or failure. *Our attitude toward life determines life's attitude toward us.* A friend of mine used to dread vacations, starting off each year's holiday already knowing that "Vacations are invariably spoiled by rotten travel arrangements and quarreling kids. This one won't be any different. You come back more exhausted than before you started. You can't wait to get back to work, to rest up!" You might guess how his vacations typically turned out. One woman entered my class dubiously, saying, "I've done a lot of work on myself already, and I haven't seen many changes to show for it. I can't say I expect to get much out of this class, either." Once you make a statement like this, you have an investment in proving your point. (Fortunately, later in the class this individual was able to make a gigantic leap in her awareness, and move from intellectualizing to acting!)

Picture the person who starts out to lose weight by saying, "I've tried every diet there ever was, and nothing works. I've been fat all my life—it's just my cross to bear, I guess." This person is defeated before even beginning. Contrast this approach with the dieter who begins by asserting confidently, "I am a thin person weighing 125 pounds. I love eating thin!"

If you radiate an attitude of well-being and self-confidence, you will be well-off and self-confident. It all starts with choosing a winning attitude.

Look for the learning in every situation. Someone once said, "I never met a person I couldn't learn something from." Search for the learning—you will benefit where others merely complain.

A woman named Donna was inwardly agonizing as she was shown to her hotel room in a city two hundred miles from her home. She had driven there to be present at her son's hearing. He had been arrested for narcotics possession, and Donna was angry at having to procure a room and practically chaperone her adult son until his appearance in court the following day. Suddenly the bell captain interrupted her angry ruminations: "You know, it must make you feel good every moment of your day that your child is the most important thing to you."

"You're right!" Donna realized. "I was feeling so weighted down with these problems, I had forgotten my priorities. This stranger has brought me back to what's most important—my love for my son, and being there to make sure he gets the help he needs." Donna then turned her outlook on the situation from negative to positive.

Unloading the victim, freeing the inner child, completing unfinished business and looking for the learning are all important steps for building the attitude that will make your dream a reality. Your winner's attitude will be further strengthened by adopting the following stances.

BE COMMITTED

Do whatever you say you're going to do. You can't believe in yourself if you don't honor your own word! Your integrity is all-important to one person in particular: *you*. You need to be able to trust that your resolve is not going to falter when the going gets tough, that you are determined to do whatever it takes to reach your goals.

STRIVE FOR EXCELLENCE IN ALL YOU DO

Stop for a minute now, to consider just what *excellence* means to you. In what one area of your life have you come closest to experiencing true excellence? How did this come about? What other experiences came close? Interview several people to get their ideas about the concept of excellence. Perhaps as a teenager you kept your very first car finely tuned and spotless. Perhaps you have sewn a garment using only the finest of materials, and you painstakingly took out and re-did each seam until it was perfect. Have you ever gone over each crevice and corner of your house with a toothbrush, until no speck of dirt remained? This is an assignment I sometimes give to enhance a person's awareness of excellence.

One woman elaborated upon this idea: "Excellence is what you learn when you study the piano as a child. When you're first learning to play, you know just three notes, and all your pieces use only those notes. They are all in the key of C. Before long, you've learned the rest of the notes and you can play in several different time signatures as well. You learn the keys of F and G. Then one day you're playing along, and it occurs to you that it's not such a struggle as it used to be. You're playing well, and you feel good about it.

"Your pieces grow progressively more complex. You practice and practice, until you get every note just perfect—even the sharps or flats. Your teacher says, 'Good! Now let me hear it again with a crescendo here, and a slight ritard in this measure.' It's a little difficult at first, thinking of all those things at once, but you manage. She says, 'Much better! Now you're ready to add the pedal here, and here, and notice these phrase markings? Try it like this!'

"You keep working, learning more and more complexities. You study stylistic variations, practice arpeggios and scales in five octaves and three kinds of minor keys. You build a repertory of sonatas and fugues, preludes and polonaises.

"One day, you sit down to play the concerto you've been working so hard on, and you forget about all those years of deatils—the music just flows forth from your heart through your fingers. You have transcended mastery, and gone beyond to the ultimate point of it all—sheer, uninhibited creative expression. The discipline was necessary; all that work had to be done first, to bring you to that point of pure excellence."

You may be fortunate enough to have had such an experience of excellence, too—maybe in one of the arts, or in a field of sports. But I find it rare to meet someone who has actually pursued excellence to the extent of knowing it as an intimate friend. And yet if your dream is a big dream, and if you want your life to work on the high level that you say you do, there's no way around doing the work it takes to get you there. Dreams are not about mediocrity.

What Is Excellence to You?

So now turn to your Dream Book, and take a half hour or more to write about your understanding of excellence. Then make a list of areas in which you will need to develop excellence to live your dream. Write what steps you will need to take, to achieve excellence in each area.

Think of yourself as a person who is wildly successful in the areas you wish to be, when you are living your dream. Will that success require excellence in specialized skills? In time management, or in managing people? In personal presentation? In communication skills? In typing or computers? In a foreign language? In accounting or law? In managing your home and family optimally? Consider your particular needs for excellence as you write.

A fun-loving young man in a workshop I designed once challenged me: "I work in a stockroom here at the supply depot. It's always a mess there. You've got to be kidding if you think *this* place could be run on excellence!" I said, "Well, I'm not sure about the whole place, but I do know that *you* could take responsibility for bringing excellence into *your* own experience." Russ good-humoredly took this on as his personal mission. He would come to each session with delight to report, "Did you see any trash in the hallway on your way into this room? Well, there sure was, before *I* came in early and picked it up!"

Russ began making dramatic entrances into the company lunchroom, announcing, "I'm here to clean this place up!" and soon others became more conscious about their surroundings. He put up a sign in his work area: "I'm taking care of my job—are you taking care of yours?"

"I got it!" he said. "It's about *me* creating it, myself!"

Ellen was, by choice, a full-time homemaker. Her top priority was creating a wonderful home that nourished, supported and stimulated her family. Ellen had been a talented teacher in the past, and she made it her goal to achieve the same degree of excellence as a homemaker. Ellen loved participating in the learning process of her children—seeing them experience success after the hard, determined struggle, and awakening their delight in learning the intricate secrets of their world—names of all the backyard birds and wildflowers in the woods, six original recipes using strawberries from the garden. Ellen's attitude of enthusiasm and excellence brought energy and joy to everyone who knew her and her children.

When you strive for excellence, you will inspire others, and it will give you zest and vitality to remain steady in the pursuit of your dream.

AFFIRMATIONS EMPOWER YOUR DREAM

A winning attitude often takes work to develop. An important part of this work involves forming positive statements about yourself to replace old, negative, self-defeating thoughts. As a baby, you happily went about doing whatever babies do—touching, tasting, exploring, learning. You were without thoughts about what you could or couldn't do, so you tried many things. Very soon, a caretaking adult undoubtedly intervened, giving you messages like "Good boy!" "What a bright girl!" "No, no—naughty." We accepted these statements unquestioningly.

Over time, as we hear such statements repeatedly, we develop beliefs about ourselves, and begin to organize them into a belief system. Various experiences reinforce them and we begin to adapt our behavior to conform to them. If you were repeatedly praised as a bright child, you began to believe you *were* a bright child. Your young mind worked overtime, coming up with new ways to show how bright you were, and to elicit further praise.

In the process of living in that premise, your experience of yourself as bright broadened and took root. Soon there was no longer any question about it in your mind. You probably *still* think of yourself as a bright child, unless at some point that belief was challenged and you deliberately reevaluated it.

This is the way beliefs are formed and assimilated. As a child, it was a rather haphazard experience—our beliefs about ourselves depended to a great extent on circumstances and the beliefs of others close to us. As adults, however, we have the power to originate beliefs of our own choice. We can replace negative, limiting beliefs about ourselves with freshly chosen alternatives. We can get rid of beliefs that don't support us. In fact, to live our dream fully, a new belief system that enables us to be our best is a necessity. Our old beliefs got us this far; new ones will take us into the future of our dream.

To adopt new beliefs, we can now systematically choose affirming statements, then consciously live in them. They will become increasingly true, until we are certain that that's who we are.

So begin by taking a closer look at the way affirmations are formed. An affirmation is a firm, positive sentence designed to convey a message from your conscious to your subconscious mind. It asserts something you know is true, even though it may not have manifested in your life yet. When the subconscious mind receives this message, it goes to work on a subconscious level to align with it and bring it about.

An effective affirmation must always be in first person (I), and the present tense, and must be stated positively, not negatively. So instead of, "I will not catch a cold and be sick tomorrow" (which would focus your mind on the idea of sickness), you could say: "I am radiantly healthy now. My body feels wonderful! I see myself performing beautifully in my dance recital." Now you have replaced the negative thought with a positive, colorful image. Since the mind can only hold one thought at a time, the thought of sickness is gone, and your subconscious mind has grabbed hold of the healthy idea and has swung into action creating health.

The best affirmations are short and powerful—not wordy and intellectual. The intensity of the conviction and feeling in which they are spoken sets them in motion.

CREATE YOUR OWN AFFIRMATIONS TO EMPOWER YOUR DREAM

Now create some self-empowering affirmations for your daily use. You will need (at least) ten 3" x 5" index cards. Begin by looking over your clearing-out exercises and other work in your Dream Book so far. What positive statements do you want to focus on? Say, for example, you realized that you allow your friends to stand in the way of your career—they distract you from doing your work. You might write an affirmation: "My friends lovingly support me in my successful career." Avoid saying, "Ben and Carla support me." It doesn't work to assume that your thought could control another person's behavior. If you are tired of fighting with your spouse, as another example, you might write, not "Geneva stops fighting with me now," but: "Peace and harmony pervade my home." Or, "My differences with others are resolved peacefully, so everyone wins." Or even, "Our love is stronger than our differences. Love finds a way."

Here are some sample affirmations that students in my classes have found valuable.

I am choosing activities that support me in living my dream.

I am a self-made millionaire!

Doing what I love makes me rich.

I am earning, saving and contributing more money than I ever dreamed possible! NOW!

I bring forth the best in myself and others at all times.

I have my new job, it's wonderful, and I love it.

I take the steps necessary to handle whatever needs to be handled.

I am a naturally thin person.

I *feel* what I am feeling, now!

My feelings tell me what I really want, instantly. I can trust my feelings to help me make sound decisions.

I am powerful.

The next step for my highest expression in my life is visible and accessible to me now.

My relationships grow more honest and more intimate every day.

Write ten affirmations of your own, each on a separate index card. Put them up in a prominent place, such as on your mirror or refrigerator, or carry them with you, and say them out loud every morning and evening—with feeling. Imagine and visualize your affirmations as true for you. Practice focusing your mental energy on these truths, rather than on the way things might look to you before they manifest. Develop and solidify your belief in yourself at your best.

In summary, these are the basics of a winning attitude:

• Approach any challenge with self-confidence and a positive outlook.

- Look for the learning in every life experience, and find a way to benefit from your challenges and difficulties.

- Ask yourself, "What is the best I have to give?" and then give it.

- Choose integrity without exception—no question on this one.

- Commit to excellence.

- Work on your winning attitude using daily affirmations.

With your winning attitude, you will become your own best motivator and your own best friend. Your winning attitude can make the difference between feeling overwhelmed or rising confidently to meet the challenges and greet the opportunities you must face along the road to your dream.

So keep up the good work!

Dream Work Checklist

- Teach the "victim" to take responsibility.

- Let the child in you come out to play.

- Be committed to completing things.

- Celebrate completion!

- Build a winning attitude.

- Read your affirmations each morning and night.

- Call your dream partner. You are a dream doctor: give your partner a prescription for the next week, to help move toward his or her dream.

- Each day when you call your partner, reinforce each other for your progress and your completions. Share your accomplishments and whether you carried through with your scheduled plan.

- Keep up the mirror image conversations every morning.

- Put your Dream Board up and look at it often. Add to it as your dreams grow.

- Continue visualizing twice daily—see yourself living your dream.

- Continue daily scheduling, recording your plan for each day, what you want out of the day, and note your successes in carrying out your plan.

4

Taking Inventory and Taking Charge

Destiny is not a matter of chance;
It is a matter of choice.
It is not a thing to be waited for;
It is a thing to be achieved.

—William Jennings Bryan

THE GROUND HAS BEEN prepared, the seed sown, and germinating just beneath the surface lies the beginning of your future. Like the farmer, you are continuing to water that seed, nourish it, and protect it from disturbance or invasion in the vulnerable stages of its early development to ensure its hardy growth. You are cultivating your dream.

CRYSTALLIZE YOUR PROGRESS

Go back into your Dream Book, now, to crystallize on paper the progress you have made. Read the following questions, then close your eyes and review your learning. Then write thoughtful answers that sum up your experience with living your dream so far.

- What did I learn from creating my Dream Boards?

- What did I learn from working with my coach?

- What did I learn from writing in my Dream Book?

- What did I learn from my mirror image conversations?

- What have I learned from my daily scheduling?

- What have I learned about the blockages I create in my life?

With these sorts of questions we can finally achieve peace with our past.

The nineteenth-century writer Elbert Hubbard said, "A failure is a man who has blundered but is not able to cash in on his experiences." Everyone experiences failure from time to time, but engrossing ourselves in the experience of failure only prevents us from moving beyond it to the learning. So as you begin the process of taking personal inventory of yourself, *look for the learning.*

In the next step of living your dream, you will have an opportunity to analyze your most basic characteristics and relate them to your unfolding dream. You can move from scheduling one day at a time to long-term and even lifetime planning. Where you want to go and how long it will take to get there is up to you. Remember, you are in charge. If your dream is to become a doctor, that may take more time than someone whose dream is to scale Mt. Everest. If your dream is "to tell the total truth," it may or may not take very long. Whatever it is, your process of self-actualizing can only occur to the extent that you *know* yourself.

YOUR VALUES

You behave in the world *as* your values. Your values are not something you can lie about. Your values are probably obvious to those around you, even if they remain undefined in your mind. They are the premise from which you operate. They are inherent in how you present yourself, and in that which you aspire to and actually do.

WHAT DO YOU VALUE? WHAT DOES YOUR LIFE SAY?

Begin by looking at many dimensions of the topic of values. You can explore what your core values are, and how your value system affects your ability to live your dream. Here's a survey to reveal what your *life* says you value. Take a few minutes to write brief answers to the following questions:

- What do you find yourself doing most often?

- How do you spend your time?

- What do you talk about?

- What do you do when you have a day off?

- What offends your sense of justice and provokes indignation and outrage?

- Which of your values are you the most proud of?

- If you set out to select the values that would best help you realize your dream, what would they be?

I once opened a fortune cookie that read, "Pay attention to what is *done*, not what is *said*." This idea has struck with me for years, making me increasingly aware of my own actions. I also began to realize that whatever I pay attention to is what is important to me. It is what I *actually* value, even though it may not always be what I think I value.

I am walking down the grocery aisle, and my hand reaches out and "autonomously" picks up a large bag of sour cream-flavored potato chips. I do want to be thin, and I have been working at choosing low-calorie foods—really, I have—but the appeal is irresistible. At this point, what do I actually value?

You can develop conscious awareness by training yourself to observe your own actions and thought processes. At that point, you begin to reclaim the power of choice over your life. A person defines and redefines who they are by the choices they make, minute-to-minute. And your choices are usually related to what you value.

Begin now to sort out and identify what your real values are. First, take a look at what you have always declared your values to be. Is there one overriding principle, such as integrity or loyalty to your friends, on which you would (and perhaps already did) stake your life and everything you own? Is there a line you would never step over, no matter what? How would you complete the sentence, "Under no condition would I ever _____"?

Alcoholics who have recovered will say clearly what that line is for them: "I cannot take a single drink of alcohol, ever again." Survivors of Hitler's war camps have described finding themselves reduced to a single absolute truth—the only thing standing between them and death was their inner conviction of their own human dignity.

What is the closest you have come to confronting *your* ultimate truth? Have you faced the extreme test of what you stand for? If so, stop now to write about your conclusions in your Dream Book. Our ultimate experiences often mark our strongest realizations about ourselves.

The answer to the question of "What would I do in the extreme test?" may remain largely an unknown to you, if you have never actually come face-to-face with a life-threatening ordeal. You may have wondered idly whether you would command the strength of character to give up your seat in the lifeboat to a child, or if lost in a desert, share your last precious drops of water. But even if you are never put to the final test, knowing what ideals you aspire to is important in establishing your value system.

My favorite photograph of myself—the one that comes closest to picturing me as I love to think of myself—shows me as a three-year-old with my hands thrown out, twirling in the wind. When I first started examining my values, I realized that self-expression was a top one for me. I could not live without the freedom to express. Relating this to my life, I knew I could not be in meetings where I was told to sit down and shut up. I could not operate in an oppressive system. I could not be around people who didn't appreciate my spontaneity.

By identifying self-expression as a top value, I saw that I would have to go back to school, to learn to express myself in the best way possible. And if I anticipated expressing myself on television, that would mean I'd want to present a thin, healthy image. So I'd have to get to work on that, too. If I woke up in the morning with a thought, "I'm tired. Let's take the day off," I might consult my values and receive the information that "You may not be able to do that, if you want to be out there expressing yourself—just press through the tiredness and keep going." So more and more, I make my choices out of my values. I monitor myself according to my values. Our values establish for us a strong, unwavering course to sail.

WHAT IS YOUR CORE VALUE?

Take your Dream Book now, and explore as you write: What is the single most important value I stand for in my life? In what ways do I demonstrate this? What value is at the core of my reason for being? What concrete actions have I taken in the past week that show the importance I give to this value? How does this value fit into living my dream?

Throughout each day in smaller ways, our values do receive countless tests. Like the tempting bag of potato chips, our small decisions add up to a major statement of what our real values are. What value statement have your decisions of the past five minutes made? Well, if you have been busily reading this book and contemplating your values, that would tell me that you take your own growth seriously, and that you have a high level of commitment to living your dream. If your mind wandered, and other intrusions entered in to claim your attention, what might that suggest?

YOUR MOST IMPORTANT VALUES: ARE YOU TRUE TO THEM?

Now list your most important values. (Note that the values you list are for right now; in ten years, or even in ten minutes, your values—and the priority you give to them—may change.) Copy your list onto a loose sheet of paper, and put it up in a place where you will notice it often in the coming week. For each action you take during the day, ask yourself if you are living out of your values. Ask, "Am I getting dressed out of my values? Am I opening the refrigerator out of my values? Am I driving in this heavy traffic out of my values? Am I getting into bed out of my values?" *Live in the question* of which values you are choosing.

Log Your Value Choices

Then, to really hone in on your daily value choices, keep a log for one week, noticing and writing about what your choices reveal about your values. At the end of the week, review what you have written and write a summary statement about what you learned. Have you crossed any values off your list? What work is needed to bring yourself into alignment with your values?

Are you excited yet? This work is powerful in its potential effects. You may be moved to question some very basic aspects of the life you have created for yourself. It may raise some discomfort, or even outright fear. If that happens, pay attention to it. What does it mean? What message is there for you? What will you choose to do?

Meaningful changes often come out of this work. A characteristic realization is, "My values haven't changed in years! Maybe since I was born. I had never consciously sorted through them and made my own independent choices."

Only by living true to your values can you live true to yourself. Without values, your life will lack focus and clarity—like lobbing a tennis ball back and forth across the net, but not really playing tennis. With your values clearly in place, your tennis game has boundaries and rules, and you can score points and be penalized for faults. Hitting the ball assumes purpose and intention. You have an investment in the well-placed serve and the skillful return. You know when you're winning.

Socrates drank the hemlock to remain true to his values. Gandhi went to prison; Martin Luther King Jr. died in the service of his values. Mother Teresa chooses a life in poverty to honor her values. Perhaps the measure of our greatness lies in conforming our lives to the values we espouse.

The exercises that follow can help you discover more about the values that are most important to you.

Choosing and Re-choosing Your Values

Read over the list of values below, making check marks next to those that are particularly important to you. Take your Dream Book, and copy down the values you have marked and add to them to make your own list.

I VALUE:

Integrity	Freedom	Wisdom
Meaningful Work	Inner Peace	Humor
Nature	Spirituality	Order
Intelligence	Fitness	Excellence
Learning	Competence	Trust
Spontaneity	Creativity	Economy
Simplicity	Self-expression	Comfort
Relationships	Companionship	Service to Others
Faith	Balance	Love
Beauty	Power	
Security	Self-discipline	

Now go over your list, and select the *five* most important values in your life as it is right now. Then write a short paragraph explaining how you chose those five.

Next, consider what top five values you would choose if your most important priority were to bring your dream into reality. What would you need to value most highly, to make your dream possible? Write another paragraph explaining these choices and discussing what changes you would make in your current lifestyle. When you have completed this work, keep it in front of you as you return to your regular daily activities.

EVERY THOUGHT COUNTS

For the next thirty minutes, observe your thoughts. Keep a tally sheet, counting the number of thoughts you have that support the values you listed, and the number that do not. Are you living out of the values your dream represents?

Make Your Own Honor Roll

Take five blank sheets of paper now, and write one of your most important values on the top of each, as a heading. Tape these on a wall or on the refrigerator. Over the next three days, consciously direct your attention to observing what your actual values are. Catch yourself making choices that agree with and support your values. Each time you do, list it on the corresponding page. At the end of the three-day period, spend some time with your Dream Book writing what you have observed. One woman said, "When I figured out the values I wanted to live by, I realized I had spent the last two days without ever giving them a thought! I want to be more cognizant of my choices." How did your lists turn out? Are your actions consistent with what you say you value? What have you learned about your values?

Strengthen a Value

This exercise can provide valuable input whenever you begin to feel off balance and out of harmony with yourself. Simply select one value to focus on, post your blank page and begin listing what you do. Here's an example from a day's entries written by Nick, a young man who wanted to build his self-confidence by learning to handle everyday tasks and business opportunities more competently.

Competence

- Cleaned every speck of corrosion from around the bathroom faucets when I shaved—ultra-perfectionism!

- Read the camera manual, so I can feel competent about operating all the adjustments and know how to take the best picture under any circumstance.

- Took extra care changing the baby. No need to feel any doubt about my competence to do simple chores like that!

- Asked my client for a more detailed description of exactly what he wanted, then checked its availability through several outlets. Drew up an exacting proposal outlining how we could optimally meet the client's needs at a competitive price.

- Cleaned off my desk. I'm on top of everything now.

- Fit in a brisk walk after lunch, so I would feel alert in the staff conference.

The attention he gave to recording these incidents went a long way toward increasing Nick's sense of being able to function competently in his world. Here's another list compiled by Nick several weeks later, when he decided that life had become too serious, and he wanted more laughter and fun.

Humor

- Got some old "Three Stooges" videos from the library.

- Read jokes to the kids at storytime.

- Started spreading jokes among the crew at work.

- Got everybody around the office telling funny things that have happened to them.

- Started looking for something to laugh about in every serious situation.

- Went with Seri to an improvisational comedy theater where we laughed our heads off.

You can imagine that Nick's list, and putting his focus on the value of humor, helped him to feel less serious and laugh.

LIVE YOUR VALUES

Now, use the information you have gathered about your values. For the next week, consciously choose to live according to your values. This may mean pausing just as you start to leap into a gossip session, by remembering your value of integrity. It may mean wiping away those crumbs and straightening up the mess instead of walking away from it, as you remember your value of neatness and order. It may mean forcing yourself to take a break from the job to relax and honor the value you place on leisure time, or writing play time into your busy work schedule.

Observe exactly what you do or don't do in accordance with your values. Observe your ideas, actions, thoughts. Gloria identified intimacy, health, honesty and service as among her top values. She placed these foremost in her mind as she went through an entire week. The first thing she noticed was how often she entertained thoughts she was unwilling to share with her husband, and how rarely she was open enough to tell him how she really felt. She began watching herself go through the rituals of play-acting intimacy, while simultaneously being aware that her mind was still revolving around the previous evening's conflict.

At this point, Gloria stopped to ask herself squarely, "Is intimacy really one of my top values? From what I'm doing, I wonder if it's not just the *appearance* of intimacy that I seek. Maybe I've been fooling myself about intimacy all along. Should I select another, truer value, and stop pretending?"

Finally, she decided that intimacy really *was* important to her, and that she would have to be more honest with *herself*, as well as with her husband. Rather than censoring her ill-intentioned thoughts, then, she began using their appearance to indicate moments when she needed to be more honest. She also realized that she had to respect her own feelings before she could be intimate with anyone else, and that sharing worries and angry feelings brings real intimacy—not play-acting the "perfect wife." Simultaneously, her health improved and her blood pressure went down. She found herself offering her service to the community in a lighter, more joyful spirit, as well.

Communicate about Values

Like Gloria's, your values are also continuously evolving as your understanding grows. The first conflicts of young adults seeking independence from their parents often arise out of the questioning of values. Clashing value systems can leave lasting rifts between parent and child. If this is true for you, here's another valuable exercise: go to your Dream Book and write a dialogue between yourself and your mother and father on the subject of values. Try to appreciate their values, and explain your values to them. Tell them how your values have changed since you were a child. Work to arrive at each person's being able to accept the other's values, without needing to change them. Write a statement summarizing the acceptance you have achieved.

Kristina's dream was to be a writer. In analyzing what it would take, she wrote to herself in her Dream Book, "You say you want to be a writer. But whenever your husband comes in, you immediately shift your whole focus away from your work, onto meeting his expectations and needs. I'm beginning to see that the result of this self-betrayal is a lot of anger and tears." Kristina came to class reporting, "Before I looked at this, I was just depressed. I thought of suicide. I saw no other way out. Now, my desire to live true to myself is stronger than my impulse to give up."

Kristina began to select values that would support her success as a writer. She decided that to be self-employed she would have to value her own time at least as highly as any other employer would. As her own employer, she would expect herself to produce a reasonable quantity and quality of work. She would hold herself accountable for a specified number of hours per week on the job and a committed level of performance. Self-discipline would be important, along with assertiveness and improved communication with her husband. At the same time, she would need to value responsible management of her time, so that she could ensure at least one hour daily for reading and research, four hours a week for sending out manuscript queries, and two hours a day of quiet, uninterrupted solitude dedicated to pure creative thought.

Kristina was surprised to discover that her husband could get along quite well without her hovering solicitous attention, and that he also was excited about helping her live her dream.

Forty-two-year-old Deanne reported, "I've been saying all along that I value money, but I have resisted doing everything that would bring in money. I guess I wanted to believe I could value *spending* money without having to be responsible for *earning* it! Today, I got the usual invitations—'How about going to lunch?' etc., and you know what I said? I set aside my impulsive self that has been getting me in trouble and replied, 'I'd love to, but I've decided to start taking my value of making money more seriously. This work's got to get done. Thanks, anyway.' And I went right back to the job without a backward look!"

Bill had a successful law practice that he described modestly as "what I do for my income." Every spare minute he devoted to tending his exquisite orchid collection and to traveling. When he settled into defining what his values were, Bill began by exclaiming, "I'm a total hypocrite!" He was overwhelmed by the guilt he felt about the time he "wasted," "puttering around" in his garden.

In probing what he actually valued, Bill discovered, "I know what it is! It's *balance*. Gardening represents my creativity—the side of myself that I have to suppress during the long hours of poring over volumes of legal precedents and carrying out routine legal proceedings. It makes sense to incorporate balance into my life."

VALUE YOUR DREAM

Have you identified what your *real* values are? Do you value your *dream*? Have you decided which values you need at the core of your commitment to live your dream? What are you going to need to value, to live a dream like yours? Post these values prominently where you will notice them often. Write about ways you will demonstrate your values to the world. Noticing and recording your values on a continual basis will ensure that you continue to empower yourself to live your dream.

When you decide to go the full distance for your dream, know that your shift may take time. It may mean going back to school, or going for personal counseling to clear away the blocks from your past. It may take setting three different alarm clocks around your house or buying a telephone answering machine to screen your calls. There is no easy way around the work that has to be done. What are the steps you need to take? Begin by defining them.

Reach Out and Ask

Reach out and ask for the help you need. Each day for a week, ask your coach to support you with questions like, "How were you true to your values today? How can you be true to your values tomorrow?" Actively practice living in congruence with what you value—today and every day.

STAYING MOTIVATED—TAKE CHARGE NOW

In Chapter 1, we began to explore what your most powerful motivators are. Now, let's take a look at two different kinds of motivation, to identify what characterizes the most potent motivators, and then find out how motivators are related to our values.

In my experience as an educator, I continually noticed two different learning approaches among children in the classroom. One child will approach every project with a vitality that is self-nourishing and self-propelling; another will sit passively and wait, asking, "Teacher, now what do I do?" This child rarely takes the initiative, depending on others for direction and waiting to be told what to do next. When a project is completed, this child looks first to the teacher for rewards and approval, whereas the self-directed child obtains great satisfaction from completing the project successfully. The teacher's acknowledgment is almost superfluous to the self-motivated child. Both children may end up learning the same basic information, but the self-directed child has gained a boost in independence and self-esteem in the process, while the other-directed child has further reinforced his or her own dependency and feelings of inadequacy.

When your motivation comes from within, you are self-directed and self-fulfilling. Your efforts proceed with focus toward goals that bring their own inherent reinforcements. You may seek others' opinions, but you won't rely on their direction before you make any move of your own. You don't have to go to somebody else to find out, "Am I good enough?" Your sense of certainty comes from yourself, not from anyone else. You don't have to wait for your spouse to "let" you do what you choose as important for your own growth; or for your parents to finally give their approval of you; or for "permission" from your friends to set out in a direction you know is right for you. You, not someone else, are responsible for making the choices that bring your good to you.

Have you ever started down a cafeteria line knowing what you felt like eating, but after you saw the special for the day, and that super-appealing dessert, you ended up buying a meal that wasn't what you wanted at all? Did you notice how unsatisfying it was? The afterthought probably occurred to you, "Why didn't I trust my own intuition in the first place?"

When you go shopping for clothes, do you get a clear picture of what you want first—or do you find yourself purchasing whatever you see that is appealing or on sale, and getting home without having found the one thing you especially needed? Do you keep your house clean because *you* like it clean, or based on someone else's opinions or expectations? Accomplishing the same task can bring, on the one hand, satisfaction and fulfillment or, on the other, powerlessness and resentment.

Other-directed motivation is based on the need to be right, to gain approval, reward or recognition from someone else, or the fear of punishment or of commitment. Inner-directed motivation is based on a love for self and others, desire for the highest good for everyone concerned, a satisfaction in one's own accomplishments and learning, making a contribution for the sake of giving without expecting direct returns, and willingly assuming responsibility for creating the outcome you desire.

WHERE DOES YOUR MOTIVATION COME FROM?

Look over the values list you just completed. Which of your top five values involve inner-directed motivators? Which involve other-directed motivators? What do you think about this? Write your thoughts in your Dream Book.

Louise began looking at her top values by considering whether *freedom* was inner– or outer–directed. "Basically," she thought, "my desire for freedom comes from somewhere inside. My spirit soars when I feel free. I am creative, natural, *alive*! I love the exhilaration of freedom, and I would do almost anything for it. I feel constricted when others impose their rules on me. If I am reacting against someone's trying to inhibit my freedom, I might misinterpret this as being other-directed at the time, but afterward I would realize that my core commitment to freedom comes from within. Were it not for that, I'd have no basis for reacting at all. Freedom is a strong inner-directed motivator for me."

Looking next at another of her top values, Louise surprised herself by deciding that *sex*, for her, involved mainly other-directed motivation. Sex was satisfying occasionally, but the main reason she had given it high priority on her values list was because through sex, she hoped to "earn" the approval she longed to receive for her physical body. Seeing this opened up a whole series of further realizations for Louise. "No wonder my relationships with men seem to end before much of anything comes of them. I haven't been honest (another one of my values, incidentally!) with myself about what I really wanted— approval. And I have been asking men to give me something I could not give to myself—a sense of being approved of, physically. This actually counteracts my value of freedom, as well, because I could never feel really free as long as I was always out to buy approval with my body!" Louise decided to choose *approval* as an inner motivator, instead, and to direct her energy into actions that made her feel good about herself.

RE-DIRECT YOUR MOTIVATION

What choices can you make to increase inner-directed motivation? Would you associate inner-directed motivation with selfishness, or not? Write your thoughts about this, also.

CHOOSE AND RE-CHOOSE YOUR MOTIVATORS

Next, read the following paragraph, and then close your eyes to imagine yourself in the scenario it portrays.

The big day has finally arrived. You know that these last five years of training are about to pay off, as you are a top-ranked contender in the Boston Marathon today. Your training has been relentless and you are completely ready now, and eager for the race to begin. There it is—the call for the line-up! Events proceed from then on in a blur, with every cell in your body and brain focused on making the best move to keep on going strong, concentrating on the course, flying toward the finish line. Suddenly, in a roar of applause and a flash of bright lights and colors, it's over. You won! You put your ability to the supreme test, and victory is yours. As if in a dream, you move around through the crowd receiving congratulations. You drink in the rewards; you revel in the glory of success. What you love most about the whole thing is _____. What you can hardly wait to have now is _____. What makes it all worthwhile is _____.

As you replay this scene in your mind, allow the full-blown feelings and sensations of the event to emerge, and see what motivates you. When you are ready, begin to write a list of "What Motivates Me Most."

Here's another scenario for you to imagine: You are strolling along a secluded riverbank. The weather is perfect: a huge azure sky with cotton-pillow clouds hovers over the green meadow on the opposite bank. Blossoming dogwood and weeping willow trees bend over the clear, lightly rippled water. "This is the life," you muse. "Everything I've ever wanted to experience is mine now. I have _____. I love _____. _____ feels so good!"

Again, allow the pleasurable and enjoyable feelings of this scene to remind you of rewards that are motivating for you. Recall the experience of feelings that you prize, sensations you would travel to the ends of the earth to claim as your own. Write about your insights in your Dream Book.

Too many people, if pressed, would have to admit that *pain* is one of their primary motivators. We sit on a hornet's nest until it becomes too uncomfortable to stay there anymore. When the dysfunction in our relationship becomes intolerable; when the clutter, sickness, disintegration or dishonesty we are embroiled in becomes unbearable— we are finally pushed to our limit, and only then do we act to bring about a change.

I asked one young man who had taken my class how his dream was progressing. He responded, "Let's face it, I'm a hopeless procrastinator." "So, is that what you want your tombstone to say?" I asked in reply. If so, then he was moving in the direction he wanted to go. If not, then what was he going to do about it?

Eleanor is a woman who came to me for some private coaching, frustrated after having spent three years undergoing professional counseling without significant improvement in her condition. She told me that all she learned was that she was depressed. She had picked up a label to pin on her symptoms, and she had even come to understand some of the dynamics of her depression—but she continued to *be* depressed.

"But," I asked, "is this what you want?" "No, of course not," she replied with some surprise. "Then let's identify what it is that depresses you, and what your options are in those areas. Let's also identify the times when you are *not* feeling depressed, and find out what you can do to create more of *those* times for yourself, right now."

Eleanor disclosed that her depression originated when her mother began living with her. The most obvious option, finding another place for her mother to live, seemed impossible to her, which was why she felt blocked. "Is there a way for your mother to remain with you without your continuing to be depressed about it?" We began to explore the types of adjustments and communications that would help clear up problems in the arrangement. Was she willing to make the changes necessary to eliminate the causes of her depression? That was still an important question. But in the meantime, I encouraged her to do more of the activities that made her feel good.

"You don't have to wait until all your problems are solved before you begin building the healthy self you want to develop," I said. "Why don't you decide to start taking some definite action to bring increased happiness into your life right now? People sometimes don't realize that you *can* do both simultaneously."

It is a principle of metaphysics that whatever you put your energy into will increase in your experience. Perhaps you have had an injury that hurt so much you could hardly stand it. Then someone distracted you or your interest was caught up by something outside yourself. Later, you became aware that you had spent quite some time without ever giving a single thought to your pain. But the minute you went back to it, the pain grew progressively worse and worse. In this way, pain can be the motivator that draws our attention to what we *don't* want. But rather than focusing on the pain and fostering its escalation, why not start right now to focus on what we *do* want? We do have the option of allowing positive, satisfying rewards to be the motivators we choose.

As parents, we often interject motivating influences into our child-rearing strategies. "You can't go outside to play until your room is cleaned up," we say. "If you sit very quietly in church, we'll go to the park afterwards." We may design a chart and put stars up on it to reinforce desired behaviors. When we become adults, it's up to us to become the nurturing parent to ourselves. We must make sure there are plenty of gold stars to reward the behaviors we want to encourage in ourselves.

"What do you like to do when you're feeling good, not depressed?" I asked Eleanor. "When I'm going for a bike ride out in the sunshine—that always lifts my spirits. Or when I go to a really good play." "And when did you last do those things?" was my next question. "Six years ago," she said.

Eleanor's example is instructive because we all have a tendency to forget to build the reinforcing rewards into our daily life that help us feel good. Once Eleanor built some rewards into her life, her attitude and perspective changed, and her depression lifted. Life is now a joyful journey for her.

So ask yourself now: What kind of rewards or reinforcers motivate you? What "carrot" will keep you running tirelessly around the track? Do you work for the money? For the chance to play? For the sheer joy of personal achievement? For applause and recognition? My strongest motivator is the joy of being able to go to sleep knowing I've done the very best I could today, and will tomorrow, too. Make a list in your Dream Book of your personal positive motivators.

A woman named Wendy was a highly successful executive in a multinational sales firm. She was midway through the "Live Your Dream" series when she received a promotion to a top-level position in Japan. Identifying her motivators was essential to Wendy's gathering the inner strength this new position would require of her. She could not afford to allow her energy to be scattered, and she must know where to plug in to get her batteries recharged. She probed deep within, until she came to an inner assurance about her source of motivation. Here's what she learned: "It's not about money, for me. It's not about prestige or titles. Now I'll finally have the position where I can *give my all* as a successful businesswoman. It's *me being in love with myself.*"

My friend the "procrastinator" decided that he was motivated by a sense of accomplishment. He realized that scheduling the hours of his day and making a list of everything he accomplished that day would motivate him to stop procrastinating and get to work. The next time I visited his office, I noted that one whole wall was covered with several weeks' worth of lists showing what he had accomplished each day. Every time he looked up, he felt rewarded and motivated anew. I didn't have to ask what he was doing to realize his dream: it was written all over the wall. "Let's face it, I'm too busy living my dream and becoming world-famous to have any time for procrastination," he joked.

Build More Motivators into Your Life

There are many other techniques for motivating yourself. You may say to yourself, "I will not leave the office until everything is cleared off this desk tonight," or, "Just twenty more pages, then I can take a coffee break." One of the most effective methods is to ask someone to support you living your dream. Ask your dream coach to call you and offer frequent encouragement and reminders. I know of a real estate salesman who promised to take his family camping every time he made a sale; his children became enthusiastic supporters of his success at work.

Following are some other ways people in my classes have chosen to build more motivators into their everyday lives:

- Exercise daily.

- Put up notes around the house to remind myself to put first things (my dream) first.

- Treat myself to more walks on the beach.

- Set aside time each day just for myself.

- Play motivational tapes while I'm driving.

- Meditate daily.

- Buy myself flowers.

- Plan mini-vacations to reward small milestones.

Successful people do not spend a lot of time sitting around waiting for the phone to ring, for someone else to come and pump them up, or for the needed inspiration to carry on. Neither do they pretend they require no motivators and no support. They take charge, in this area as in others, of anticipating and providing for their own needs. Building motivators into your life is a powerful way of assuring that your dream will receive the ongoing nourishment it needs, especially when the going gets tough, or you are under pressure or stress. So go back into your Dream Book now, and write your personal plan for making those rewards that motivate you a part of the realization of your dream.

PINPOINT WHAT YOUR NATURAL GIFTS AND TALENTS ARE

So far in this in-depth personal inventory, you have been challenged to identify what values you esteem and what your motivators are. As you work in these areas, you will find yourself moving closer and closer to knowing for sure *who* you truly are. You will begin living in harmony with the real inside *you*. Once you find it, you will want to express the real you more fully and more joyously in the world.

As you become more inner-directed, you may find yourself rejecting many of the old ways of expressing yourself that were based on your former, limited understanding of who you are. Counselor and best-selling author Dr. Wayne Dyer says, "Would you pay a fourteen-year-old or a seventeen-year-old for advice on how to live the rest of your life? Yet most of us live our lives out of decisions we made when we were fourteen or seventeen." As you look afresh at many of your life decisions, you may want to choose new ways of being that are more congruent with your self today.

You can only be fully self-expressive when you know what your natural gifts and talents are. Identifying which talents come naturally to you is the third ingredient in consolidating a congruent you.

Have you ever admired movie stars or great musicians for the sheer naturalness of their performance? Have you envied an entertainer or teacher whose work seemed more like play because he or she loved it so much? The link you felt with that person was a connection with *your* desire to have that much joy doing whatever comes naturally to you.

On the other hand, picture those frustrated individuals who bend every ounce of willpower to climb to the top of a field in which they have little natural talent. Or the miserable person who tries against all odds to force the wrong relationship to work.

During my teaching years, I kept a sign on my office wall: WE ARE ALL GIFTED. It was a highly controversial message in a public school setting, because of its implied challenge for us as teachers: *to find and enhance the gift* in each and every child.

I have had so many adults—thirty-five, forty-five, sixty years old—come into my classes still vaguely troubled by the questions "What am I going to be when I grow up? What do I want to do with my life?" And so many who finally realized that where they've worked so hard to get is not where they want to be at all. Then it's "Oh, *no*! Do I really want to go ahead with this?" as the mounting discomfort surfaces.

So be forewarned, you may come to a stunning realization that makes you want to run back home and hide in your closet. You may be tempted to crawl back into that smaller shell of yourself where you were comfortable and secure. But if you're not living from your true self—that greater being you now know you are—you won't be living your dream.

What Do You Do Well? Acknowledge Yourself

The third part of this in-depth personal inventory can help you identify your natural gifts and talents. Begin by examining some activity you recently completed, and listing everything you can possibly think of about it to acknowledge yourself for. Acknowledge yourself for all the little things involved. For example: I got home on time (I am usually punctual—good for me!), and I took care to water all the way to the corners of the yard (I did a thorough job. I am a conscientious person who takes pride in my work). I worked quickly and efficiently, pulling out the dandelions at the same time. I interrupted the job to give my child my total attention for a few minutes (I honor my child's needs and take good care of him); then I went right back to finish the job (My ability to carry through a task to completion has grown immensely!). I respected my body and peace of mind enough to sit down and relax for ten minutes, so I'll be able to handle the demands of my family with renewed energy.

This exercise—acknowledging yourself in writing—is an effective tool in building self-esteem. Use it whenever you have a need to feel better about yourself. Try using it in situations where you feel terrible about how you've been doing—writing about all the good you can extract from your experience. Once again, you will demonstrate the magic of focusing your attention on the positive. You will experience great benefits from tending to and nurturing your self-esteem; why hang around waiting for someone else to pay you a compliment and make you feel good? This exercise also helps to identify the individual components of your natural talents and gifts—breaking down broad skills and abilities into specific elements.

When you use your most natural curiosities, strengths and talents, you can grow and express yourself powerfully and effortlessly. In contrast, if you are trying to force yourself to become good at something that goes against your grain, you are likely to struggle every inch of the way. You may be able to succeed—but how much more successful might you be at something that comes naturally to you! Discovering exactly what your natural gifts are—and are not—is crucial to maximizing your potential.

Identify What Comes Naturally

What do you bring into the world that is uniquely you, that is yours alone to give, that is your mission? Let's return to take a closer look at who you were as a very young child, as well as who you are now. In your Dream Book, write quick answers to these questions, applying them to the earliest age you can remember.

- What did you like to do most as a young child? Did you build bridges or block towers? (A cousin of mine used to play at building bridges and "traveling" all over—he grew up to become a state highway engineer responsible for designing beautiful transportation systems and bridges.) Were you the entertainer? Did you put on plays or performances? Did you direct them? Did you feel most alive when you were playing a role? Were you the farmer? Planner? Organizer? Teacher? Peacemaker?

- What words did you use to ask questions? Did you want to know *why* or *how*? Were you curious about how things worked, or were you more interested in explaining the mysteries of life, or in finding out what made up the tiny parts of a flower or weed? Did you want to understand people, or nature, or intellectual concepts, or mechanical objects? What truths were you already intuitively certain about, even as a child?

- What were you good at? At home? In school?

- What are you good at now? Are you a detail person, a troubleshooter, an administrator? Are you exceptionally good at getting along with people? Can you bring out the best in others, or make them feel at ease and appreciated? Are you skilled at enrolling others in projects you initiate? Do you run a tight ship or give great parties? List twenty things you do very well. Break each activity down to identify within it what the separate components are that you particularly enjoy. (Note: This list will be most beneficial if you continue to add to it and modify it on an ongoing basis.)

- What makes you feel most alive? List five experiences you've had recently when you felt vitally alive. Beside each, identify *what* it was about the experience that made you feel so good.

- When do you feel most highly energized? List five activities that give you so much energy nothing else matters when you're doing them. You forget about time, and about being tired or hungry or bored or lonely, you become so engrossed.

- Recall two experiences you've had lately when you felt absolute joy. Write *how* you brought this about.

When do you feel the happiest? As a natural teacher, I feel my greatest joy when someone, out of my guidance, is growing and becoming more of who they are.

A woman named Anna listed cooking as one of her skills. Breaking down the experience of cooking into more specific details, Anna wrote:

"I love to create new dishes and modify recipes I find, to improve them and make them unusual. I love to invent stimulating mixes of new flavors, colors, textures—the *artistry* of food preparation. I enjoy being the agent of transformation, as raw materials are turned into exquisite culinary creations. I enjoy testing myself at handling routine procedures simultaneously and efficiently—the organizational aspect of it. I love the compliments I get about how wonderful my cooking is. I feel a sort of detached amazement that '*I* did this!' followed by a self-affirming, 'But of course—I *am* good!' And . . . I love to taste my creations myself. I even enjoy the satisfaction of seeing all the pots and pans and mess cleaned up and put away afterwards. And I like giving people the feeling of being specially cared for."

When Anna looked back over her writing, she realized how important being an artist and a creator were to her. She also knew her gifts were stimulated and rewarded most in a social context, and she would not be happy as, say, an isolated studio artist. She noted that managing events and the details of a production was an experience she relished. Integrating these conclusions with those she drew from writing about other activities helped Anna develop a clearer picture of herself.

Another woman I know discovered her ideal career by a process of exploration similar to the one above. Larita came up with several specific characteristics she would want to express in the perfect job. It would be one where her critical mind would be an asset, one in which she could bring her varied experience together, keep learning and read a lot, be creative, decide independently how to spend her time. When she had listed all this, Larita could not imagine such a job. She set her list aside and went on as usual with her job search. But within two years, she found herself in an editing position that miraculously combined all these different aspects.

If you are seeking greater career satisfaction, take some time now to prepare a similar list of your ideal requirements. Out of your answers to the questions above and previously, write the characteristics your ideal career position will have. Be sure to mention ways in which your natural talents and skills will be used.

Another way of identifying your natural gifts is to take a survey of fifteen people who know you. Ask them questions such as, "What am I good at? What do you think my talents and skills are?" As you receive their responses, write them down. Take some time to consider the feedback you receive, appreciating that *you* are still the world's foremost authority on yourself, and that you will be the ultimate judge of its validity. Ask yourself, "Is that true for me? Does this person see something I overlooked?"

PUT YOUR VALUES, MOTIVATORS AND TALENTS TO WORK FOR YOU

Having inventoried your values, motivators and talents, you are now ready to take charge and put this information to use. The next step is to develop a plan for accomplishing your dreams.

Develop Your Dream Plan

Begin by setting aside eight pages in your Dream Book and writing one of the following titles on each page:

- Physical Body

- Relationships

- Career

- Work and Home Environment

- Mental State of Being

- Spiritual Life

- Financial Well-Being

- Leisure/Recreation

Now, on each page, down the left-hand side, write these headings:

My Ideal Self, in:

- My Entire Lifetime

- 10 Years

- 5 Years

- 1 Year

- 6 Months

- 3 Months

Whenever someone calls me a "dreamer," I smile, because I know it is true. I also know that the other side of dreaming the dream is that I am willing to do the work needed to bring the dream into reality. This is the point where many people get stuck. The dream must be translated into quantifiable stages and manageable tasks, which must be accomplished one step at a time. It may take time and hard work, and it is unlikely to come about by magic or fervent wishfulness.

Magic will sometimes happen, but a step-by-step plan may be needed as well.

If your dream is to get a college degree, the steps you must take are laid out for you in advance. You will take the required classes the first year, do all the homework and term papers, and pass the exams. You will be thinking about choosing a major area of interest. Advisors are there to guide you along the way and answer your questions.

But what if another part of your dream is to have ever-present peace of mind? What classes can you take? If there is no established program, you may have to design one of your own. This may involve experimenting to find ways that will work for you. It may mean false starts and regrouping for a renewed drive. Your game tactics and strategies will need to be reviewed and updated often, as new information comes in and new directions are chosen.

I am always excited whenever someone discovers, "Well, my dream is not what I thought it was." This says to me that they are moving deeper and deeper into themselves. Often, the way we zero in on our dream is to state what we believe our dream to be right now, start working on it, and learn as we get there that "That's not it, but now I'm closer to knowing what it *is*."

Knowing that it's never possible to produce a final, set-in-concrete plan, we must start where we are right now to develop a flexible, working model for accomplishing each part of our dream. As in most human enterprises, the thinking and planning stages are vital to successfully realizing the result. Consider carefully: are you willing to do this work? If not, when will you be? What will happen if you put it off until later?

When you are ready to take your commitment to your dream onward, turn to the first of the eight Dream Plan pages that you have prepared—the one titled Physical Body. Look back at your Dream Boards and the other work you have completed so far, and make a list of the aspects of your dream that relate to your physical body. You might want to include your ideal health, weight, appearance and exercise program. For each item, decide what actions and results you intend to accomplish within a ten-year, five-year, one-year, six-month and three-month time period. Note specific dates, so you can refer back to them and gauge how well you're meeting your projected schedule. Your first page might look something like this:

My Dream Self: Physical Body   Today's Date: 6/1/89

TIME	WEIGH	RESULT	ACTION
Lifetime	125 lb.	Radiant health.	Exercise or walk daily.
10 Years By 6/1/99	125 lb.	Free of allergies.	Reach goal of climbing Mt. Kilimanjaro.
5 Years By 6/1/94	125 lb.	Sneezing and difficulty breathing all in the past —breathing free and clear all the time.	Hike Mts. Shasta and Rainier.
1 Year By 6/1/90	125 lb.	Install air filtering system.	Train for mountain climbing.
6 Months By 12/1/89	150 lb.	By 11/1: Decrease red meat to twice a week; continue allergy treatment regimen.	Join athletic club by 11/1; start mountain climbing classes.
3 Months By 7/1 By 8/1 By 9/1	165 lb. 160 lb. 155 lb.	By 9/15: appointment with allergist; vacuum for dust twice weekly.	Aerobic dance class three times a week.

Here are two sample pages I developed as a plan for realizing the mental and spiritual aspects of my dream:

My Dream Self: Mental State of Being   Today's Date: 1/1/89

TIME	RESULT	ACTION
Lifetime	To have expanded my creative, intuitive and logical powers to maximum capacity. To acquire a vast familiarity with the accumulated knowledge and culture of the ages, and to develop the wisdom and understanding of a sage.	Read from great books of the world daily. Attend cultural events twice a month. Cultivate friendships with wise people from all over the world, and continue in my journaling to seek inner guidance in making wise life decisions.

10 Years By 1/1/99	Gain expertise in various world cultures through study, classes, and cultural involvement, being a learner as well as a teacher.	Guide anthropological expedition to Zaire; visit the foreign minister and bestow museum endowment for preservation of Zairian artifacts and culture.
	Identify principles of "Live Your Dream" found in other cultural heritages, and discover myths and folk tales teaching these principles.	Teach "Live Your Dream" in many countries, adapting it skillfully to incorporate appropriate cultural variations.
5 Years By 1/1/94	Have greatly expanded horizons and contacts. Increase my information continually, and become a meaningful contributor.	Travel to Switzerland and Italy. Cultivate friends who are experts in many fields. Select an organization and become a substantial contributing member. Purchase the Great Books series and encyclopedia; read daily.
1 Year By 1/1/90	Increase my formal and informal education.	Subscribe to mini-lecture series at the university; acquire collection of music tapes and art reprints representative of many cultures; take music appreciation and art history classes.
6 Months By 7/1/89	Attend six cultural events and read five books. Become informed about world travel and begin planning first trip.	Start a book review group meeting twice monthly. Research travel arrangements and contact travel agent.

TIME	RESULT	ACTION
3 Months By 4/1/89	Select an area that I know nothing about, and write a list of books I want to read to become knowledgeable in that area.	Take a travel preparatory class on Europe.

My Dream Self: Spiritual Life   Today's Date: 1/1/89

TIME	RESULT	ACTION
Lifetime	Turn over all decisions to a Higher Power. Be living my life at the total state of acceptance. Become a transcended master. Be prepared to celebrate the death cycle as part of the life cycle and to meet my Maker in peace.	Be masterfully powerful.
10 Years By 1/1/99	Establish such a strong connection with my Source that others are empowered. Be a channel of divine empowerment.	Go public with my message—television and radio worldwide.
5 Years By 1/1/94	Demonstrate that I am empowered by an unlimited Source.	Give talks; facilitate workshops sourced by Higher Power.
1 Year By 1/1/90	Experience joy at will. Passion for life is my motivating force.	Meditate daily, opening myself to more and greater joy, love, inspiration.
6 Months By 7/1/89	Turn everything over to God—of free choice, not just in desperation. Get myself out of the way.	Keep a record of my successes each time I turn something over.
	Write what I will do based on my daily log.	Take action indicated by my writing.

3 Months By 4/1/89	Develop awareness of what my fears are of trusting in a Higher Power, and of the choices I make—to trust or panic.	Keep a daily log of my trusting and doubting thoughts. Record the amounts of time I spend on creative, trusting solutions vs. time spent on doubting. Read inspirational books and listen to tapes daily.

Visualize End Results

Continue completing your remaining Dream Plan pages in this same way. When you have finished, you may wish to combine the information you have compiled and display it in a vivid visual way. One of my strategies has been: after identifying clearly what I want to accomplish, I imagine seeing my result in the highest corner of every room I walk into.

Try creating a personal graphic design that will represent your Dream Plan at a glance. You might develop a flow chart, cluster drawing, tree or yellow brick road—or think of a different design, uniquely your own! Let your imagination go, release your creativity and really have fun with this.

Keep It Current

The very fact that you have now stated your Dream Plan and identified its working stages has set in motion the process of realizing your dream. As you continue doing the work necessary to keep to your schedule, look at your Dream Plan periodically. You may decide to change parts of your dream or of the stages and steps you have plotted along its course. You will undoubtedly be astonished at the progress you have made, if you truly commit yourself to each aspect of your dream.

And watch out! Your life may change! You will uncover possibilities and potential you never knew you had. You will discover all you were meant to be. You will *become* your dream.

Dream Work Checklist

- Spend fifteen minutes daily visualizing yourself living your dream, and write your thoughts in your Dream Book.

- Keep reading your affirmations, morning and night.

- Make a list of the steps you've taken so far toward realizing your dream. List completed items, steps accomplished in them, successes and milestones.

- Live according to your values. Pay attention to whether you are doing this or not.

- Build inner-directed motivators into your everyday life.

- Acknowledge yourself often, and deliberately build your self-esteem. Acknowledge others, too.

- Think about and list activities that bring you joy and aliveness.

- Work with your dream coach to repeatedly drill each other on the question, "What are you best at?" Give quick, spontaneous responses—whatever pops into your mind.

- Add one item every day to your list of natural gifts and talents.

- Outline the specifications of your ideal job.

- Create your Dream Plan, and begin work on it.

- Create an imaginative visual display showing the steps and stages of your Dream Plan.

- Call your dream coach five times a week and ask how you can assist him or her in living according to their values. Share what motivators are influencing you right now, and ask about your coach's Dream Plan progress.

5

Your Power to Turn Negatives into Positives

> There is no such thing as a problem
> without a gift for you in its hands. You
> seek problems because you need their
> gifts.
>
> —Richard Bach, *Illusions*

PROBLEMS OR challenges appear in our lives from time to time. There are days when everything seems to be going wrong, and we proclaim with exasperation, "You'll never prove to *me* that any good is coming out of this!" Yet we can look so objectively at the lives of others and see that it's not the *problem* that can make or break you; it is *what you make of it.*

Do you make mountains out of molehills, or do you make mole-hills out of mountains? Do you look at your difficulties with appreciation or regret? In this chapter, you will have an opportunity to practice techniques that can enable you to make the most of every situation you're involved in. Turning a handicap into a victory is the stuff from which heroes are made—you've seen the movies, read the books, dreamed some of the same dreams—and you can do it, too, from one moment to the next, starting now.

Challenges often do turn into growth experiences. Charlene, a woman who had been married for fourteen years, was faced with the shock of her husband's leaving her suddenly for another woman. Never having worked seriously to earn a living, and being responsible for the support of three rebellious teenagers and an expensive home—did she view this as a positive opportunity in her life? She certainly did not—at first. But within six months, she had identified a career goal and found a job that would sustain her while she took night classes to get a degree. She had even enlisted the aid of her children and developed her family into a cooperative unit, all helping out through this difficult time.

Charlene began to be deeply appreciative and excited about the new life that was opening up to her. Suddenly, she recognized how stifled and bored she had been before, and how reluctant to make changes in her too-comfortable life. What had seemed a tragedy evolved into a new, much more fulfilling life for Charlene.

LOOK BEYOND THE STRUGGLE

Is it time for you to stop suffering and struggling, to relax and peacefully accept a change, and turn your energy into making your problem situation into a winning one? In your Dream Book, write answers to the following questions.

- What useful purpose does my suffering and resistance to change serve?

- Do I need it to grow stronger in some way?

- Do I learn *more*, the harder I struggle and suffer?

Someone once said, "What is our pain but the breaking of the shell that encloses our understanding?" We can try to clutch at the pieces of the shell as it crumbles around us, or we can leap out and go exploring in a new world.

Vicki Noble, author of *Motherpeace,* captured this idea beautifully when she wrote, "The destruction of the old always precedes the building of the new, but one can choose which side to be on." Which side do you want to choose? If you feel like you're being dragged along, kicking and screaming, in the currents of change, looking for the gift in the situation may be the last thing in the world you want to do. Or is it? Once you begin to reach toward the light at the end of the tunnel, your attachment to the swirling confusion around you loosens. And the faster you can change your focus, the less you will ever feel yourself at the mercy of life's events.

A kite rises against, not with, the wind. Opposition is often what teaches us. Conflict wakes us up. Have you ever noticed with surprise that you had actually *chosen* a problem as a way of motivating yourself?

A young man named Andrew encouraged his wife, "Go ahead. Take that acting class in New York, if that's what you want to do." The moment she was gone, however, he found himself engulfed in doubt and paralyzing loneliness. He knew that *she* was growing and changing. Things could not go on any longer as they had been.

Without his wife, Andrew realized it was up to him to get himself motivated. Finally, staring into the mirror, he came to a powerful conclusion: *I don't like myself like this—how could anyone else like me? I've got to make some changes. It's either grow or die!"*

Andrew had begun his week feeling lonely, deserted, helpless and clinging. He and his wife had avoided being apart with a fervor unmatched in many of their other endeavors. To his credit, Andrew was able to use this opportunity to break out of his pattern of dependency. He ended the week having faced the truth about himself for the first time in years. He was ready to make some changes.

Another person who was jarred by a problem into making some unanticipated changes is Bev. Bev lived in a beautiful large condominium in an expensive area of town. But her life-style was really more luxurious than she could afford. As the bills began mounting up and she was forced to evaluate her finances, Bev realized she could not pay such high rent. She went through an agonizing struggle. Where would she go? What could she do? Would she be able to find a place she liked?

"I had to move," she said, "and when I didn't find a place by the end of the month, I made a decision that freed me, temporarily, from all the doubts and questions. I put all my possessions into storage, packed my three kids and dog into the car, and drove to Salt Lake City where I had once lived. There we were able to stay with friends and I could continue my consulting work, until I could save enough money to come back home.

"The comfort of being with friends who cared, and getting away from it all, gave me the freedom I needed to think things over. 'Exactly what do I want?,' I kept asking myself. Once I knew that, I could make a plan for getting it. Before long, we were able to return home and rent a small apartment in a very low-budget section of town. There we put up with midnight brawls in the street just outside our window, and every day I drove the kids all the way to the other side of the city so they could attend their old school—until, finally, I saved enough to move back to the area we loved.

"Out of this adventure, I was able to find a small, modest but wonderful house which is perfect for us, right in my old neighborhood! I had been content before in the big condo, and I might never have thought of moving. But now I am happier than ever in my new, perfect little house—and the whole experience has been invaluable in teaching me to be clear about what I really want—and to live within my means."

TAKE A THIRD-PARTY VIEW

I often encourage people to write about a problem as if it were someone else's story. This has proven to be a valuable technique for turning negatives into positives. After you've completed "your story," read it over several times. With the detachment of an uninvolved third party, you may be able to see your situation from a new perspective. Ask yourself, "What am I learning from this problem? What advice might I give to someone else facing these circumstances?" Write several feedback sentences for yourself.

Go into your Dream Book now, and take some time to write about three problem situations presently going on in your life. As soon as you finish, call your dream coach or a friend, and share your insights.

The third-person view is also a valuable technique to use when you decide it's time to understand unresolved issues you experienced as a child. Try testing the exercise now. Recall several childhood memories, and write each as "someone else's story." Work with a memory that seems to block you from realizing a dream you have. As you write, keep in mind that the goal of this exercise is to turn what seemed to be negative into a positive. Like an author who already has planned a story's plot, mold your story to reach the conclusion: what a *gift* that "problem" was!

There is always a gift in the problem situation. We turn our problems into opportunities when we allow ourselves to stop struggling, let down our resistance and graciously accept the gift.

Gwen's ego felt defeated when she lost the election to the state senate seat—a goal she had given up a dedicated legal career to pursue. The campaign had been a hard and bitter one, and her opponent's smear tactics had churned up rough water for her to tread. Months later, she looked back on the outcome with gratitude. Working as a political science professor was much better suited to her nature, she now saw clearly. And her election experiences had broadened her knowledge of the field immeasurably. Every graduate of her class had passed through an in-depth exploration of ethical campaign practices.

THE POWER OF YOUR DREAM TO WEATHER THE STORM

As you move toward becoming your dream, you will unavoidably find that everything in your life that is *not* like your dream will come up for you to handle. We often create some rain, to give ourselves a little time to get ready for the changes we must face. We clear away the storm by riveting our eyes firmly on the rainbow of our dream, and moving steadfastly through the clouds.

I used to visit my grandchildren in a seaport village where it was foggy and rainy most of the time. Every time I planned a visit, I would tell the children, "Now, I love warm, sunny days. So let's know that we'll have a sunny day when I come." They would hold the thought, "The sun is shining for the good of all concerned. And *we want that now*." And when I arrived, the weather was miraculously beautiful. One day little Cathy told her preschool class, "My grandma *is* the sun!"

I have found Cathy's belief in me and in herself to be very empowering. The truth is, *we all are the sun*—when we move right through the clouds and rain to the clear skies beyond.

The way out of the rain clouds is to start asking questions. *If I create the storm, what purpose is it serving for me now? What can I learn? What is to be gained from the difficulty I must face? What do I need to do, to clear away the storm and bring out the sun?*

A young man named Joseph followed his dream through a tempestuous storm to the clearing beyond. In his early thirties, Joseph discovered that he had always wanted to move far out into the country and farm his own land. When he decided at last to make this major change in his life, he began at once to look for suitable properties. His hopes were soon dashed by the discovery that he was already too far in debt to qualify for the essential loan. "I just can't do it," he thought. "It's too late. There's no way." The storm moved in.

But one sunny morning he remembered that he knew how to make good use of his problems. He began asking the questions necessary to discover the learning in the dilemma he faced. Soon the realization dawned about what he would have to learn and do: In order to be able to trust himself with owning his own farm, he had to build up credibility with himself that he could be financially responsible. He had to learn to keep tight control of his spending, and to channel his resources into his most important purposes.

It might take a few years of concentrated effort, but he would use the time to work hard and pay off all his past debts. In the meantime, he could take agricultural extension classes, learn the business aspects of farm management and prepare himself in many ways to embark successfully on his new life. When he was finally able to buy his farm, Joseph made the move much better equipped to succeed than if he had done so impulsively three years earlier.

FINDING THE ELUSIVE GIFT

The gift in the problem situation is sometimes obvious, other times not. The athlete who sprains an ankle misses the championship competition, and is thus spared the agony of defeat or the challenges success might bring; the person who missed the plane that crashed; the person whose arrest for drunk driving channels him into a rehabilitation program; the flat tire on the way to a meeting you hated having to attend; the failure of a qualifying exam for a field that is stifling—often, such experiences give us clarity about what we really want.

Our resistance to receiving the gift usually comes from clinging to a different result. The gift only becomes available once we let go, release our expectations that things *should* be different, and open ourselves to the learning.

A Formula for Release

Here's another technique to release yourself from being stuck in a problem, and help you find its gift instead. Use the following list of questions—either ask your coach to read them to you and tape record the answers, or work on your own, writing the answers in your Dream Book. You may find this method valuable for many issues now and in the future.

- What is bothering me?

- What are the effects of this issue on me—mentally, physically and emotionally?

- What is the effect of the issue on those around me?

- What does the issue cause me to do or not do?

- What are the advantages of these effects, with respect to living my dream?

- What are the disadvantages of these effects, with respect to living my dream?

- How would life be different if the issue were gone?

- Why do I need the issue?

- What beliefs do I have that explain how this issue might have developed?

- What are the payoffs for keeping the status quo regarding this issue?

One dreamer gave the following answers to these questions. Note how her discoveries unfolded.

- *What is bothering me?* Most of all, it's the fear that I won't have enough money to pay my bills as the first of the month rolls around.

- *What are the effects of this issue on me?* Well, mentally, it has me worrying a lot. I go over and over in my mind, what could I do if this or that happened? What else could I possibly give up or do without, if I have to? What's the worst scenario? My attention seems riveted to the problems. Emotionally and spiritually, I withdraw into myself and my fears. I'm not able to do the creative work I need to do, and this aggravates the problem further, because when I'm more productive, I make more money.

- *What are the effects of this issue on others?* As I isolate my-self, my children feel abandoned and worried also. Their behavior gets worse, making my life even more difficult. Friends I could turn to for help or understanding see me as distant and aloof, so they leave me alone.

- *What does the issue cause me to do or not do?* Because of my preoccupied fear, I become very cautious about taking any risks. I get into the survival mode, leaving the creative mode behind. I make calculated judgments based on minimizing my losses—rather than saying what I want and just going af-ter it. I don't go to professional seminars that would help me to advance in my career. My holding back extends to my so-cial life and leisure time, as well. I don't laugh, or dance, or play, or go outside and enjoy myself as much. I feel afraid and tense.

- *What are the advantages of these effects, with respect to living my dream?* Well, I suppose I could think of a few. For one thing, I am more careful not to waste money. I am forced to choose what's most important to spend my money on and eliminate the less important activities and purchases. That keeps me focused, with less scattering of attention and resources. I know I can't afford not to get my work done, so I push myself harder. I take my responsibilities more seri-ously, and I am more independent.

- *What are the disadvantages of these effects, with respect to liv-ing my dream?* I feel burdened, not free. My energy is con-stricted. I am troubled that I'm not being the role model I want my kids to have. I'm stewing in lack and limitation, while I'm telling my daughter to pull out all the stops, go to college and become a doctor. Most of all, I tend to forget about my *dream* altogether, I'm so caught up in dealing with one problem after another!

- *How would life be different if the issue were gone?* Simple! I'd go out and do all the things I want to do, buy all the things I want to buy, stop worrying, and get out there and live my dream! (Of course, I don't know if I'd be *as* productive, or push myself quite so hard. Maybe I'd be lazy, if I didn't *have* to worry so much about the money.)

- *Why do I need the issue?* Now that'a a hard one. Let me think. . . . Maybe I have to prove to myself that I can be trusted. And that I can handle it all—I am strong. I weathered the storm. Maybe, even, a little self-righteousness: one day I'll look at all the people who underestimated me and say, "I told you so!" Also, as I said before, it helps keep me motivated and moving. On the other hand, maybe I *don't* actually *need* this issue at all! Maybe I could accomplish what I want without it, now that I see what my choices are!

- *What beliefs do I have that explain how this issue might have developed?* Several come to mind:

    You have to work *hard* for what you get.

    You can't have it all—you have to choose.

    There's barely enough to go around.

    Why would you deserve so much—think of all the starving children in India!

  Having low self-worth probably explains it more than anything else. I grew up not thinking very highly of myself and my abilities. I didn't expect to be worth a lot of money. I tend to undervalue myself and my work.

- *What are the payoffs for keeping the status quo?* As long as I'm always struggling to keep my head above water, I don't have to face the challenge of becoming greater than my little, personal struggle. I have some fears about becoming a highly successful person, being out in the world in a bigger way. What if you skip way out on a limb, and then it breaks? That's an even greater risk than clawing your way up the tree and clinging to its trunk. So I'm protected, in a sense, from bigger failure, by playing a smaller game.

My worrying also serves to keep me focused on building my business. I have to keep choosing what's important to me. I have to be responsible and accountable. I'm practicing the policies I need to master to succeed in a bigger way. Also, there are some things I need to get cleared up before I will be ready to make it in a really big way.

You know what I just figured out? This issue that I have been considering such a big, heavy problem is actually quite useful to me in many ways. By going through all this, I can see that looking at it in this new way will help a lot. It's a challenge I will face and learn from; why not make it an adventure, a divine comedy, instead of a morbid tragedy? It's my chance to handle my concerns about money, once and for all. You know, the more I trust and let go, the more confident I become that I can trust still more in the future.

This person worked with her problem until she was able to transform it into an opportunity. She moved her energy state from problem-solving into dream-creating. She has her eye on the rainbow now, and the dark clouds of doubt are but a veil to be drawn back, exposing the bright light behind.

As long as you stay stuck in your problem, it's very likely that your subconscious mind will send out commands to every function of your body and mind: "All right—all forces—align with the block! All forces, align with the depression." The switch comes when you take over the controls and send out an overriding command: "All forces, align with the solution. All forces, set your sights on my dream!"

WHAT'S THE PAYOFF?

Payoffs often represent an important part of our unwillingness to make a desired change or to resolve an issue that troubles us.

Payoffs are often insidious—we may have difficulty even identifying what they are—but that doesn't weaken their power over us.

Our payoffs for staying stuck can be many and varied. We may enjoy the camaraderie of the down-and-outers. We can hold a "pity party," commiserating and accumulating sympathy about how *bad* it is, and how awful so-and-so has been acting. Have you ever noticed how talking about a situation may divert your attention from taking any action to remedy it? At worst, we can even aggravate the situation by dwelling on and magnifying its negatives.

Yet, we sometimes go from one person to the next, dumping our story onto anyone who is willing to carry around some of our bad feelings for us. It doesn't help them, and it certainly doesn't help us resolve our situation, either. The answer? Take care to release your energy not into puddles here and there where it will only stagnate and ferment, but into constructive channels where it can go to work for you and solve the problem.

Frequently, our payoff in staying with a problem is that we simply choose to remain safe and comfortable, rather than to take the risk of change. The appeal of a regular paycheck, pension plan and health insurance certainly made me hesitate to leave my secure teaching position to expand my frontiers.

Another payoff might be that as long as you're focusing all your energy on outside problems, you don't have to be the main character in your own story: someone else is responsible. Someone else is to blame. You can observe what is happening to you, and just *react*, rather than *act*.

Write and Rewrite Your Story

Brett was a student who gained insight into his pattern of reacting rather than acting. I suggested that he write a short story about his life as it would be two years from now, if his problem situation remained unchanged. "I saw my future as clear as a bell," he reported after rereading his story. "I kept getting fatter and lazier and more withdrawn, and my wife kept getting angrier, more bitter and critical. I drank more beer, and she stewed in silent protest until she exploded with rage.

"No!" he exclaimed. "I don't want my life to look like that." Brett wrote a second, parallel story about his life in two years, describing the needed changes to create it the way he wanted it.

This exercise of writing parallel stories may help you to picture the scenery along each of two diverging roads you must choose between. It also can give you the impetus you need to make your decisions for change. So take your Dream Book now, and write two stories for yourself: first, as your life will be in two years if you stay with your present problems, and second, as your life will be if you have made the needed decisions to create the life you want.

GET CLEAR AND TAKE ACTION

On the other hand, perhaps the time is not yet right for you to make your change. Your payoff may be the extra time you need to adjust, or to prepare yourself or other circumstances in your life. In this case, it may be advantageous to define what conditions you are waiting for, and be clear about *when* the time *will* be right. Perhaps you need to take some classes, research your options or interview others for their opinions. Is your dream greater than all your other considerations?

There's a fine line between knowing the time is not quite right— and procrastinating. Whenever I have doubts about taking the next step or pausing to honor my own timing, I ask the question, "Am I supposed to go, do, be that?" I take it to my Dream Book. I write the question at the top of a blank page and then sit quietly until the answers start to come. I have discovered that I am always provided with the clarity I need before I take action. Your subconscious mind always knows what the right decision is for you. Writing brings out the inner knowing.

CHOOSE HEALTHY PAYOFFS

Illness often serves as a faulty problem-solving technique. Temporarily, if you get sick, you don't have to be responsible. You can avoid communicating honestly or confronting an uncomfortable situation or relationship. You can take that much-needed rest, now that your body demands it. On top of that, you may be able to elicit someone else to take care of you and handle things for you, and perhaps even give you loving attention! And others will inquire sympathetically about your condition; then you can share sickness stories.

As director of a private elementary school, I initiated a way to accomplish all these goals—without the necessity of getting sick to do it. Our "wellness policy" was based on the principle of integrity. Every staff member and student was held responsible for creating his or her own state of well-being. If someone wanted to take a day off to work on their well-being, that was fine. The school was in full support of wellness, and we encouraged everyone to take the best possible care of themselves and do whatever they needed to provide healthy conditions for their bodies.

People were amazed by the freedom we made available to the children. I was often asked, "Will anyone ever *come* to school?" "Oh, yes," I always answered with confidence. The fact was, absenteeism was almost nonexistent in the school. The children and staff loved coming to school, and hated to miss a minute of it. We found that once you challenge people at a high level of integrity, they will respond at that level—and feel wonderful about themselves in the process.

DEVELOP YOUR OWN WELLNESS POLICY

So here's a challenge for you: develop your own wellness policy. Design a decorative page in your Dream Book, and use it to write answers to the following questions:

- How many days a year will you need to take off from work, dedicated to your well-being?

- What will you use your days for?

- Will you expect to be reimbursed for these days? How will you work out a way to be paid?

- List ways in which you will reward yourself for wellness. How will you treat yourself in a special way on your well days?

- What action will you take when body symptoms begin to send you messages that your wellness may be in jeopardy?

- How will you enroll others in your wellness?

- What arrangements will you make with your employees and co-workers, to accommodate your wellness policy?

- What will you do to enroll others in *their* own good health?

I have noticed that the only times I've ever been sick were when I was not honest about facing situations affecting me. I got laryngitis when my attempts to speak out and challenge a repressive boss failed to make an impact. If I was sick, I could not work there. Finally, I had to face the truth that that environment was not where I belonged—and leave it. I haven't had laryngitis since.

My learning from this experience was to be honest with myself and honor my own important values. Out of facing this problem, I left a job I might still be in otherwise. I opened up a whole new arena of opportunities that I never would have encountered in my old job. What a gift this has turned out to be!

Many individuals have brought wellness to triumph over illness by analyzing the payoffs of their illness and choosing more effective ways of having their needs met. Karen was dealing with the problem of obesity. When she looked at the payoffs available from being over-weight, she realized she "was letting her sandbags keep her balloon from going up." Once she decided to be a light, carefree, happy person, she began letting the excess weight fall away.

Another woman, Lynne, was troubled by a distressing skin rash that made her feel unpresentable. "What are you itching to do?" I asked her. The work she most wanted and yet feared to do involved being in the public eye. Her decision to go ahead and do it anyway marked the end of her problem with rashes.

Headaches often have the payoff of excusing people from going somewhere or doing something they don't want to do. Headaches can be replaced by a straightforward decision to honor our preferences and express them openly. We can choose to resolve the issue actively, rather than passively blocking our creative energy.

Backaches, too, may result from a person's feeling that he or she is carrying more than the fair share of a burden. Backaches can ex-press passively, "Get off my back!" A back problem may force a person to cut down on a heavy load of obligations, or to ask for needed help. Again, actively handling the situation more effectively might become the choice of preference. Some of the most powerful people I've ever met are ones who took the gift from a critical illness and turned it around.

VACATION OR HOSPITALIZATION—WHAT DO YOU REALLY WANT?

Think of the last time you felt sick. What was going on in your life? In your Dream Book, write what was going on in your life at three other times you have gotten sick. For each, write what the payoff was. Did the sickness bring about the desired payoff? Would there have been an alternative way to reach that goal? What can you learn from this?

NO MORE PROBLEMS—NOW WHAT?

Despite extensive work to get their lives in order, people frequently find themselves actively or passively sabotaging their own efforts. They catch themselves in the act of almost deliberately setting up new problems, moving backward instead of forward, throwing away the gains they have made. What can be going on? They are hard-pressed to understand.

It is a common occurrence that once we clear away the clouds and shift our focus away from solving problems, we feel a void in our lives. Something will rush in to fill this void. We'd better be ready with a plan to go forward—or else, watch out! A new problem will arise to compete for our newly freed attention.

The alternative to focusing on our problems is always to *focus on what we want*. By knowing what we want, we can:

- Design our day, just the way we want it.

- Know what we're working for and where we're going.

- Choose whom to be with.

- Set our goals to align with our larger intentions.

The quickest tool for refocusing is always the single question: "What is *your dream?*"

MOVE INTO CREATING YOUR DREAM

So once you are ready to move beyond problem-solving into creation, ask yourself:

- What do I want?

- When do I want it?

- Am I willing to take action?

- At what point will I definitely take action? (How bad does the situation have to get before I reach the absolute limit of my willingness to put up with it?)

- What possible actions could I take? (Be creative here: the more unlimited your thinking, and the more possibilities you define, the better your chances for success will be.)

- What specific actions *will* I take, by what specific times?

- How will I know when I have what I want?

- What is my payoff in *not* having what I want?

- How will I reward myself with an equal or even greater payoff for *having* what I want?

A MODEL FOR MANAGING PAYOFFS AND OPTIONS

Here's a flow chart modeled on these questions. Once you have studied it, take a blank sheet of paper and create a flow chart of your own, to help you transcend a problem situation you'd like to resolve in your life at this time.

Steps for Solving a Problem

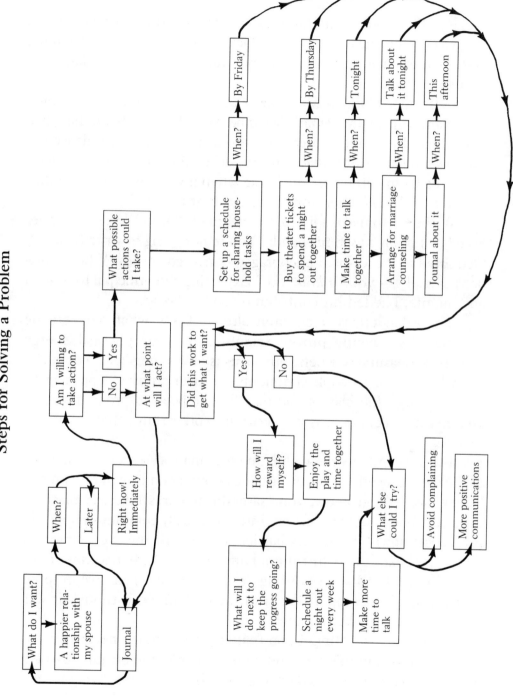

THE POWER OF YOUR WORD

Reaching your dream takes motivation, determination and effort. You will need to clear away the obstacles that have blocked you in the past. One obstacle that often escapes our awareness is the language we use.

I was once working with a class of small children when I noted how many disparaging remarks were being exchanged. Something had to be done. I initiated a discussion about the power of words we use with each other—words that make us feel better, and words that make us feel bad. One little girl said, "Like when my daddy tells me to shut up—you feel *dead* when someone says that to you."

We began to make a list on the board of "Dead Words." Another little boy timidly raised his hand: "You're not going to write this. . . ." Dedicated to the lesson, I encouraged him to go ahead. "When somebody says, 'F——— you,' it *kills* you." Expecting the principal to walk in any minute, I added his contribution to the board.

These kindergarten children already knew what bioenergetic research has recently proven scientifically: your physical energy decreases measurably when your focus is on the negative. Yet in our everyday language, people commonly use killer phrases. A participant in one of my adult classes told me, "I have been so programmed to be a negative person, it is my constant work to turn that negativity around!"

I was recently working with an older man who seemed unaware of the damaging effects his sarcasm dealt out. I confronted him on this "killer talk." "You know, your sarcastic remarks take the place of genuine, honest communication. Instead of really communicating, you put people down. It creates a barrier between us, and every time you do it, I feel like you've just put a knife in me." A change came over his presence, but I was counting on our working relationship to be strong enough to support the truth being told, even though it was painful to hear in the moment.

At our next meeting, Leon thanked me. He had never realized he used sarcasm in this way, and injuring people and creating barriers were not what he really wanted to accomplish, of course. "You already know this," he disclosed. "What I am really working on is my own low self-esteem. Thank you for helping me to see this."

The most deadly effect of killer talk is not on others, however, but on the self. When we say, "I *can't*" or "I'll *try*," we deflect the power of our intentions away from positive action and an open mind, onto negative and limiting ideas and judgments. We see ourselves as powerless.

Imagine that I say, "I *should have* stopped at the store on the way home. We *need* milk, but I *can't stand* waiting in those *unbearable* long lines at rush hour." In these two small sentences, I have heaped guilt on myself with the loaded assumptions of the word *should,* and I have judged myself as *needy* and *intolerant*. I am left feeling wrong and ineffective.

On the other hand, suppose that I say instead, "I will go to the store for milk later, to avoid wasting time standing in line at rush hour." This is a statement that empowers me: I have viewed the situation objectively and chosen my action based on my own preferences. I feel effective and in control, and I have not cast negative judgments on myself or anyone else.

If I say to you, "*Why* do you *never* call me when you're going to be late? *You are* so *inconsiderate* and *thoughtless!*"—in all likelihood, the way I have phrased my remarks will short-circuit our communication. You will be made to feel wrong, and your predictable response will be either to withdraw defensively or to counterattack. My accusations may seem justified at the moment, but my problem remains unresolved, and in the long run I will feel, once again, frustrated and ineffective.

On the other hand, I could consider more carefully what I want to communicate. I might choose caring language that invites a response: "*I felt* concerned when you didn't call. I didn't know whether to go ahead with dinner or to wait. I thought of canceling this evening's plans, but then I was sure you'd be here soon. After wavering back and forth like this, I began feeling angry. *I want* you to know what I have been going through. *I'd like* reassurance that you care about me and are concerned about what I'm feeling."

The language we use can subtly set up our experience and determine the way we view ourselves and others. Awareness is the key to a successful experience. Practice noticing the words you choose.

Enliven Your Language—Enliven Your Life

In your Dream Book, title a page "Dead Words," and the opposite page "Alive Words." Make a list of words you use and hear. Notice yourself saying:

I can't	Why didn't you . . .
I won't	You *never* . . .
I'll *try*	Don't . . .
I should have	Shame on you!
I can't stand . . .	Can't you ever . . . ?
I *need*	You *always* . . .
If only . . .	Will you *ever* learn?
It's their *fault*	You *have to* . . .
We've *got to* . . .	But . . .

If you aren't careful, you'll . . .

Practice substituting words like these:

I like	Thank you
I can	Good for you!
I will	I like the way . . .
I'll *do* it	I appreciate . . .
I want	Well done!
I feel	Nice job!
I love	I choose/choose not to
Let's talk about it	What do you want?

Become an observer of your language, and notice how you feel when you use Dead Words and Alive Words, and how you feel when other use them with you. Practice consciously choosing empowering language. You will be amazed at the power of your own words.

TURN YOUR WEAKNESSES INTO STRENGTHS

Now, let's examine and work with some other ideas you may have about yourself.

MAKE AN INVENTORY OF YOUR STRENGTHS

We'll begin by using the sentence starter, *A strength I have is.* Repeat this quickly twenty times, completing the sentence with a different ending each time. Just say the first thing that comes to mind, without stopping to think or judge your responses. Here's an example:

A strength I have is __I'm a great clarinet player.__

A strength I have is __willingness to admit my mistakes.__

A strength I have is __my athletic body.__

A strength I have is __I write wonderful letters.__

A strength I have is __a mature relationship with my parents.__

A strength I have is __my strong sense of humor.__

Go ahead now, and explore your own strengths, counting up to at least twenty completions for this sentence.

Then read this next section over carefully: it has the potential to change your life.

Usually, when I ask adults to list their strengths, they mention many skills they have mastered and things they are good at doing. I have never yet had an adult list as a strength something that he or she was still in the process of developing. Yet a child will joyfully boast, "I'm learning sign language!" or, "I want to be an artist when I grow up." As children, we see all our potential abilities as strengths. It's a wonderful outlook that need not be sacrificed on the altar of adulthood.

Benjamin Franklin once said, "A weakness is a strength not yet developed." Go ahead and make a quick list of ten things you consider to be weaknesses you have. Now, here's the trick: look at each of these "weaknesses," and begin to see it not as a weakness, but as a strength in the process of being developed—a *budding strength.*

For example, a participant in one of my classes was laid off from a long-term career position. She felt so incapacitated by fear and worry that she was unable to begin searching for a new job. Using the above procedure, she identified her weaknesses: the fear of making new contacts, of going to job interviews, of being put on the spot, of fumbling and feeling awkward and self-conscious, and presenting a miserable impression of herself and her abilities.

From these weaknesses, she wrote the following strength statements: "A strength I have is that I can go into interview situations with confidence and self-assuredly present my best self." "A strength I have is that I enjoy the opportunity to make new contacts and explore new possibilities with new employers."

"I realized I had made some arbitrary decisions about myself, and I was stuck with the consequences of them. Suddenly I knew I could instantly change those decisions—and would!" she exclaimed afterwards.

List Your Budding Strengths

So what are your budding "strengths"? Use the power of your word to turn each of your weaknesses into a strength you are now developing. Make a strength statement: "A *strength* I have is _____."

Extend Your Strengths

When you have completed your strength statements, go on to list on a separate sheet of paper every negative idea you have accumulated about your appearance, your abilities, your intelligence, your cooking, your social skills, your education—any negative thought about yourself that you have. Then use a separate page in your Dream Book. For each negative belief on your previous list, write a new, empowering strength statement. Example: "I am a clumsy, bumbling idiot" might be changed to "I am coordinated and clever." "I am terrified of talking in front of a group" could be replaced with "I am a confident, inspired and inspiring public speaker."

Eliminate Weaknesses

When you finish this list, keep it and tear up the other list of negative ideas and burn it or throw it away.

Creating positive strength statements to replace the old negative ideas and beliefs may feel at first like wearing new shoes. Your logical mind will naturally come through with all kinds of "reasonable" arguments and objections. The old beliefs were familiar and comfortable; will the new ones ever fit? "But," you may think, "I don't *feel* coordinated and clever! How can it be true?" Someone once advised me to view these thoughts like passing clouds in the sky. Just allow them to appear, and observe them as they move on by. In the meantime, go ahead and *be* your new, strengthened self.

One less constructive—and usually unconscious—thing we do with our negative self-concepts is punish ourselves for them. We use guilt and self-punishment to keep ourselves in line, and correct our "bad" behaviors. We criticize our own egos, denying ourselves pleasure, privileges, and even basic needs, all as punishment for our own perceived misdeeds or weaknesses.

Of course, self-punishment does not work. It also robs us of vitality and aliveness, and cuts us off from the reinforcing strength of feeling good about ourselves.

Always Write About Your Learning

When we punish ourselves, we turn away from the potential learning of a situation. It works far better to appreciate yourself—you did the best you knew how to do, given the circumstances and your experience to date. Your choices have led to another opportunity to learn further. *Instead of being critical, be curious.* What are you learning through this? What is the value to be derived from your experience?

Do you sometimes punish yourself? How? For what? As you progress in turning negative thoughts into positive ones, notice also when you are punishing yourself. Write about this in your Dream Book. Write how you can accomplish your purposes by loving yourself more instead of punishing yourself.

Remind Yourself to Positivize

Write yourself some reminder cards, and post them around your working and living space:

HOW IS THIS PERFECT?

WHAT AM I LEARNING AT THIS MOMENT?

DOES THE THOUGHT GOING THROUGH MY MIND RIGHT NOW SUPPORT ME IN LIVING MY DREAM?

Start shouting and chanting whatever you want to be true about yourself. Yell out in the privacy of your car, "I am a confident public speaker!" "I present material in a clear, articulate way." "I am determined to succeed."

You are the authority for your own life. You, and you alone, are the one best qualified to make all the decisions, choices and judgments on your life. So don't let people, places or things get in the way of choosing what is right for you. If I perceive something as a problem, *my perception is the problem.*

When you work from the position of your strengths, you begin to live from the full array of your potential. Your life shifts from a struggle for survival to an adventure in choosing what you want. You move out of the problem-solving mode into the creative process.

Any problem can be turned into a positive learning experience if we purposely ask ourselves, "What's the value in this situation? What is the gift? The understanding? What am I learning?" Approach your problem situations not with groans and complaints, but with a willingness to learn and receive the gift. Just say, "Oh, good! This must be perfect! Let's look at how. Might as well have fun with it." Hop over your resistance and move lightly through your next learning opportunity. You will maximize your energy and your effectiveness. Instead of choosing to be miserable, why not choose to enjoy yourself?

Are you having fun yet?

Dream Work Checklist

- Keep up your reading, and writing in your Dream Book.

- Continue completing things and working on your Dream Plan.

- Write the story of your problem from the point of view of a third person.

- Find and receive the gift in every problem situation.

- Examine your problems or issues.

- Identify the payoffs related to an issue.

- Release your energy into constructive channels.

- Write parallel stories about your life in two years.

- Write about the payoffs of illness and what your alternatives are.

- Develop your own wellness policy.

- Keep asking, "What do I want?"

- Make a flow chart plan for getting what you want.

- Watch your words—use alive, not dead, language.

- Ask your coach to catch you using Alive Words and compliment you.

- Turn your weaknesses into strengths.

- Stop punishing yourself—appreciate and learn.

- Choose to change your focus from problems to solutions.

- Turn your negatives into positives; choose to move on and enjoy!

6

Dare to Stretch and Expand

Dare: to be sufficiently courageous; to
challenge; to confront boldly; an act of
imaginative or vivacious boldness.

—Webster's Ninth New
Collegiate Dictionary

MORE STRETCHING? Yes. Is there no end? When do I get to lie back
and get comfortable and stay the same for the rest of my life?
Never. I hate it! No—I love it.

The day I decided to be all I am, I became fully aware that
stretching and expanding was to be a constant, lifelong process.
There's always more to learn and more to become. Our only limit is
our own willingness to grow.

Of course, it's important to take time off to rest, relax and reju-
venate. But overall, if you are fully committed to living your dream,
you will be working harder than ever before and enjoying it more—
having more fun than you ever dreamed was possible.

I know people who can have a good time at parties. And some
people can really enjoy their night at the ballpark, an evening out or
a weekend camping in the mountains. But how many people do you
know whom you would describe as one hundred percent *happy* individuals? Who *love* their lives, and live full-out, with gusto and without
constraint? Who through being who they are, are making a difference
in the lives of others?

This is you, if you are continuing to stretch and expand, to fill more and more of the possibilities of your dream every day and every year. When asked, "Are you having fun yet?," what is your answer? In this chapter, we will expand *fun* to *FUN!*

This is a critical point now. You are headed toward celebration. Those new shoes are being broken in—soon, they will feel so natural, you will run and dance freely in them. You will not only boogie, you may learn to dance the mazurka or compete in the Olympic high jump. You will extend your idea of what your shoes and you can do.

This is a point where many people give up, if they have not built adequate self-reinforcing rewards and supports into their program for growth. It's the point at which some people want to sit out my remaining classes as nonparticipants, while those who keep doing their homework move forward by leaps and bounds. The steps required are not always easy—*and* the rewards are incredible.

So, are you fully committed to advancing your dream? Are you ready to progress to the next level, to leave behind your reticence and excuses, and do whatever it takes?

REINFORCE YOUR LEARNING—
IT'S GETTING FUN NOW!

Begin by taking stock of your progress in stretching and expanding to live your dream so far. Start at the beginning of your Dream Book, and review what you have written. As you do this, make notes of the actual, concrete progress you have made since you began living your dream.

Reading over your work is an important way of reinforcing the steps you have taken and the leaps you have made, both in awareness and in action. Acknowledge yourself! *You*—and no one else but you— have done what needed to be done to propel yourself into your own future. What changes have you made? How is your life different now? In your Dream Book, write a summary of your "Live Your Dream" process so far. Then meet with your dream coach, and read it over to him or her.

Living your dream can be a lonely process. Your dream is *your* dream, and no one else can live it for you. And it can be scary, too.

In my work with private clients and groups, I have constantly been made aware how vitally important it is for people to keep acknowledging themselves for their progress and to create a strong support system for this purpose.

Recently I observed my youngest grandchild toddling her first steps across a living room filled with doting relatives. An appreciated child does not give up after one fall. You don't drop out in the middle of the race if you have a cheering squad behind you. What athlete makes it to the Olympics without a dedicated coach?

ENROLL A SUPPORT SYSTEM

An extremely powerful seminar I created is called "Together to the Top." Its primary function is to provide each participant with whatever support is needed to zoom to the top of his or her potential.

Having a committed support system really does work, and you may want to organize such a group for yourself. Find several people who can be counted on to give you enthusiastic encouragement. Have everyone hold constant the vision of each person's dreams through the difficult times and diversions. Agree to give each other needed nudges and positive reminders, and to tell the truth with love when it needs to be heard. Emphasize recognizing the progress each person makes—with fanfare, celebration and fun.

THE NEXT SHIFT IN CONSCIOUSNESS

Psychiatrists are sometimes disparagingly known as "shrinks," comparing the science of understanding the human mind to "head-shrinking." Presumably, a person's thoughts are so immense and unwieldy that they must be shrunk down to size to impose order on them. It is probably true that we do have to contain an untamed creature within the scope of our understanding before we can assume authority over it and teach it to do what we want.

An important step in human evolution was made when psychiatry began to be identified as mind *expanding*. Self-awareness is then associated with *expanding*, instead of contracting, our experience.

It is the awareness of our own inner dynamics that gives us the power of choice over our lives, and the power to choose to transcend old patterns.

It is through self-awareness that we can choose to be in the stretch and expand mode now, and make our next important shift in consciousness. Here are two small stories to introduce it.

The Wretched Little Old Lady

Once upon a time there was a wretched little old lady. Each morning she woke up with the very same thought—"Do I *have to* get up already?" Then she would look outside and see the leaves the wind had blown over her walk. "Do I *have to* sweep the walk again?" she would whine. Her house had a way of getting dirty overnight, it seemed. "Don't tell me I *have to* clean again today!" she moaned. She would stare resentfully at the list of bills and taxes she *had to* pay, and the garbage that had to be taken out. And the leak in the roof had to be fixed before it rained. But the one thing she hated more than anything else was the sight of all those happy faces going to and from the playground across the street. It was more than a body could bear, seeing everyone else smiling and playing, when all *she* had to do was work and worry.

The Cheerful Little Old Lady

Once upon a time there was a cheerful little old lady. Each morning she would look outside and see the leaves the wind had blown over her walk. "Oh, good!" she would exclaim. "I can sweep the walk again! What a beautiful day for being outside!" And sure enough, her house was dirty again. "It feels so good to clean," she would think to herself. "It's great exercise." When her eye fell lightly on the list of bills and taxes to be paid, she would think how much she appreciated all the people and services she was helping to support—like the trash collectors, for example. She could just leave her garbage on the curb, and it was all taken away for her. "I guess I get to learn about fixing leaky roofs next," she smiled, knowing in advance that something of value lay ahead for her in that experience. Her contented smile was reflected back in the eyes of a young passerby on the street outside.

And that's the shift we are ready to make: the shift from *I have to . . .* to *I get to. . . .* This simple shift, when entered into wholeheartedly, allows us to see ourselves as living completely from choice, one hundred percent of the time. It replaces fear, resistance and reluctance with excitement and enthusiasm. And what do you have to lose? So let's begin to put it into practice now, as you *get to* stretch and expand further into your dream!

EXPAND YOUR ENERGY

One of the most common dream deterrents you can inflict on yourself is letting things remain incomplete. This brings along guilt, lack of self-worth, lowered self-confidence, diminished energy, depression and lethargy. Have you experienced any of these feelings lately?

DECLARE YOUR FREEDOM FROM INCOMPLETES

In Chapter 3, you began to work seriously on a comprehensive list of completions. How have you been progressing on it? Turn now to that checklist, and mark any items that remain incomplete. Explore each of these items, writing about it in your Dream Book. What questions do you need to ask yourself about it? What is stopping you from completing this item? What would you have to do to complete it? Take a close look at how it is occupying a corner of your attention and using your mental energy.

I used to spend months thinking and talking about how to handle this person or that situation. When I learned to handle each thing immediately as it came up, I discovered that now I have nothing to think about except my dream! I'm no longer carrying anything along from the past. My energy is completely released to go forward.

People sometimes wait until someone dies to confront the unspoken words that remain to be communicated, deeds that were never done. We are reminded by a death how important it is to remain current in our communications and actions. But why wait? Staying current is just as important every minute and every day of our lives.

What was so amusing about Fibber McGee's closet in the old radio program "Fibber McGee and Molly"? We can't open the door of a stuffed closet without everything from the past twenty years tumbling out. But until we clean out and get rid of the unused baggage, we tend to forget that it will all fall out again, each time the door is unwarily cracked open. Once we do clean out our symbolic closets, we can open them and easily find a space for new things we acquire.

When I was working full-time and going to school, along with raising four children and remodeling our home, people used to say to me, "Gosh, you've got a lot of energy!" Many wanted to view me as a person who had been somehow specially endowed, biologically, with an exceptionally high level of energy. But there is no mystery to high energy levels—simply keep up-to-date in all your affairs and you will be constantly revitalized. Our life energy is natural in each of us. How much of your energy is free to live your dream today?

Push Beyond Excuses

Ask yourself about each unfinished item on your completion list: How will I be closer to living my dream once this is completed? Take a close look at any excuses that come to mind:

- I have to wait until I have the money.

- There'll never be anyone else, if I complete this relationship.

- Someone in my family might need it someday.

- I might fix it (fit into it) someday.

- If only my husband/wife would *ever* get around to it!

- My mother wouldn't approve.

- If I complete this, I'll have nothing left to do.

One advantage of being an educator is that I learned early on there's *always* more to learn. There are always more projects to take on, more work to do, more people to play with. So confront your excuses head-on, and recognize them for what they are—just excuses. Then get back on course with: *What do I want?*—excuses, or results?

Ask yourself: What is the push that will get me through this? Discuss it with your dream coach, letting him or her know what support you could use—a friendly reminder, praise and encouragement, assistance . . . a push?

FIND YOUR HIDDEN AGENDA

How consistent with your dream is the image you are putting out? Your hidden motives may be more obvious to others than your stated intention is. People in my classes have uncovered many unstated agendas that work in opposition to their dream. Some common ones are "I am invisible—don't notice me"; "I want to be taken care of"; "I am a rock—nothing gets to me, and I can't be hurt"; "Mr. Nice Guy"; "I'll be the victim, and you rescue me"; and "I'll save you, you poor helpless victim."

I was once at a party when someone asked a friend of mine, "How do you *live* with a husband like that, who's always the life of the party, keeping everyone in stitches?" My friend replied coolly, "I *don't* live with that person. The person *I* live with comes home from work, has a beer, plants himself in front of the television and falls asleep. This comedian? I only see him at parties."

Old Images and New

What is your hidden agenda? Do you put out a message about yourself that is unlike your dream? What is the new image you want to put out? Write several paragraphs on this in your Dream Book. An ideal method to evaluate yourself and monitor your growth is to record yourself on videotape, modeling both your hidden agenda and your new image and discussing how your new image supports your dream.

FINE-TUNE YOUR ENVIRONMENT

When I was decorating our new home, my husband asked, "Do you have to have those exact drapes? What difference does it make? Wouldn't these others be just as good?" "It makes all the difference in the world," I said. "Those are the drapes that will say to me, every time I look at them, 'Yes—you *are* living your dream.'"

When you're living your dream, everything that you say is important counts. You can't live your dream from a compromising position. Your dream demands the best of you. Every dark, dingy corner of your life makes an indelible shadow on your dream. It must be brought out into the light and cleaned.

Take a Toothbrush

You must fine-tune your life. An exercise I have found extremely valuable to many people is the assignment to take a toothbrush and a magnifying glass and scrub every corner, every crack and crevice in every room of your house. It's a discipline that teaches people to see the dirt that's always been there but never noticed or attended to. It also requires taking personal responsibility for every aspect of your surroundings. You have to be willing to own all your nooks and crannies before you can know how to own anything greater.

So get out that toothbrush, and practice developing visual acuity. Challenge yourself to find more, and then even more and more, smudges and grime—and then aggressively get them cleaned out. Take charge—it is your life you are creating!

Now, take a symbolic toothbrush to the rest of your life. Scrub out any old dirt that takes up space your dream could fill. Update your completions list and begin conquering it. If it takes *years* to complete all this work, what better way could you be spending your time? Each item you cross off your completion list frees you to live your dream.

New Beliefs for Old

Next, look back at your work from previous chapters on the habits, beliefs, persons and things you allow to stand in the way of living your dream. Look also at the things that motivate you, and your values. You can use the work you've already done to create a chart of belief statements designed to move you beyond whatever is still holding you back.

Have you noticed yet that the only thing holding you back—really—is the *idea* that something is holding you back? In other words, it is *you*. So under each category—Habits, Beliefs, Persons, Things,

Motivators, and Values—write five belief statements that tell the highest truth about you, canceling out previous ideas about whatever you thought was holding you back.

Under *People,* for example, you might write something like: "I now have loving friends who stand by me," or "People love to pay me richly for the excellent work I do." And under *Habits*: "I get up early and feel enthusiastic," or: "I eat right to support my ideal weight and health, and I feel great." Under *Values*: "I see beauty everywhere I look," or: "My leisure time is a source of joy and inspiration to me," or: "In intimate relationships, I am completely honest." Choose powerful statements that will empower you to live your dream.

Read your belief statements to your dream coach, and then continue to read them over daily, with the conviction that they are now true. These belief statements will have a very powerful effect, even thought people do not always get results overnight. It's often a gradual process. Someone will say, "I was looking back in my Dream Book at all those belief statements I wrote six months ago—and, do you know, I now have everything I included in them! I hadn't realized it before this."

People most often notice that they are now interacting in a whole different way, and no longer dealing with negative people; and that the people they spend time with have changed dramatically. Hazel was a woman with a number of paralyzing fears. She began using a belief statement: "I now have inner peace." Many classes and workshops later, she called to let me know, "I think I'm almost there!" Without giving it a second thought, she was relaxed and at ease talking on the phone—previously one of her most incapacitating phobias.

A severely depressed and suicidal woman came to see me. She began her first session stating, "I don't know *what* I want, and it doesn't really matter much anyway." As her therapy progressed, we worked together to create some new belief statements: "I love life, and life loves me." "My path becomes clearer and clearer with each step I take." "Thank God for my amazing life!"

Protesting all the while—"I don't know what the hell good this is going to do"—she began using these belief statements daily. Alicia today is a vibrantly happy woman who travels widely, writes for several newspapers, and spontaneouly shares her joy wherever she participates.

YOUR MAJOR LIFE SHIFT

Everything beyond whatever has stopped you in the past is now yours for the having. There are no more stops. Everything is there to support you in realizing your highest good, for the highest good of all.

DEFINE YOUR SHIFT

As you actualize the belief statements you are practicing, you will find yourself making a major life shift: from the person you used to be, to the person you want to become. What words would you use to describe the major life shift you are making? Are you changing "from keeping things in to giving and expressing yourself," or "from some-one who's *preparing* to someone who takes action," or "from someone who takes orders to someone who gives orders"? "From someone who sits in the bleachers to someone who plays down on the field"? "From someone who takes care of others to someone who takes just as good care of myself"?

Write your life shift in your Dream Book along with your belief statements, so you can read it every day. Add the affirmation, "I'm changing—I can feel it!"

YOUR DREAM WORKSHOP

For this next section, you will need a tape recorder and a blank tape. Plan a time when you can be undisturbed and completely without distractions. Unplug the phone, put a sign on your door, or do whatever you need to do to assure yourself this solitary time. Begin by reading the following visualization into your recorder. Some background meditation music may be played to enhance the effect. Read slowly, and leave generous pauses wherever your imagination will need time for fantasizing. When you're ready, begin:

As you work on your life shift, there is a special place you can go to build your dream. You are now going to create your own imaginary Dream Workshop. Place your Dream Book and pen close at hand to record your thoughts afterwards.

Get into a comfortable position and close your eyes. Relax. With every breath, count to ten, relaxing further until even the hairs on your arm and the tiny muscles around your mouth and stomach are relaxed into peaceful, expectant anticipation. [Pause.]

You are going for a walk down a tranquil country road. The road is lined with flowers and tall swaying grass, and oak trees with bending boughs overhead, as sunlight plays around their shadows. The atmosphere is wild with the fragrance of wild rose and honeysuckle, and you breathe in the fresh, sparkling air. Birds and squirrels whistle and chirp in harmony, as one great, joyful community of nature's creatures. Even the dust under your bare feet feels soft and clean, and a summer breeze covers you with warm caresses. You turn off onto a small path that winds up a gently sloping hill.

Drinking in the beauty of your surroundings through every pore, you begin to sense that you are arriving at a special place that is all your own. You approach an opening, and you know that once you go in, you will be in a place where you can receive any information you need to create new dreams and find complete peace.

You pause, aware that everywhere around you, you are being flooded and bathed in radiant white light. In the brilliance of this healing white light, all troubles diminish into insignificance, and you are revitalized and energized and filled with absolute love.

Now you are ready to proceed inside. You imagine the perfect entryway, a doorway that invites you to come inside and bask in the unlimited possibilities within. Perhaps it is a wooden or glass door, one that swings or slides open at the touch of a button or the glance of an eye. Create your own ideal door now. [Pause.] And go on inside.

Take a look around you: you're in a very special place. Use your imagination to make it beautiful and wonderful in every way. What are the walls made of? The floor? Are there windows? What is the view like? You turn off to one side, and notice an alcove specifically designed to be your own computer area. With a wave of your hand or push of a key, you can ask the computer any question. [Pause.]

Pay close attention as the answer is printed out: it will assist you in growing in the next step of your dream. [Pause.] Knowing that the computer will always be there, and you can go back to it any time you want, you move on to see what else there is.

Now notice what you are wearing. You can be anyone you want

here. Choose the look that best supports your dream. You walk a little farther, into another room, your video area. Here, all things are possible, and you can use your video equipment to create yourself living your dream, right there on the screen. Turn on the life-size screen now. As it lights up, you see someone appear there. Who is it? [Pause.] What do they have to say to you? [Pause.]

You notice a procession of people on the screen, all lining up to see you. Some of them are ones you used to think were stopping you from living your dream. But now, as each person comes up to greet you, they seem to have a gift for you or message to tell you. Allow each person to appear before you, and listen. What is the gift? What is the message? [Pause.]

When the last person has gone on, notice if there is anyone else you would like to call onto the screen. You can call anyone you want to this magical screen. It has no limits of time or space. You can call someone from out of your past or future, or even someone who is no longer living. Ask them anything you want, and receive the gift of their answer. [Pause.]

Look again. This screen has an even more special purpose: it can instantly enact and reenact your thoughts to create the ideal scenario of your dream. Suddenly you see, clear as life, the picture of you living your dream. [Pause.] Create a title for your very own video—see it, appearing on the screen? [Pause.] Watch as the plot unfolds. You *are* living your dream! [Pause.]

Soon, you are ready to continue on. You know that your video room will remain here for you, and you can go back any time you want.

Now it's time to prepare your special place for doing the work required to create your dream. Your work area will be as unique as you and your dream are. See that space now, exactly as it needs to be for you. [Pause.] If it needs to have a higher ceiling or a different kind of floor, build one. You're able to create anything you want, in any manner you choose. [Pause.] Is this the place you'd like to have some stained glass, or some special plants? Would you like to bring in something from nature? Snap your fingers, or wave a hand: there they are! [Pause.] Is there any special equipment you need? A piano or other musical instrument? Art supplies? Tools? You can have as much as you want. Place yourself in a perfect position for creating your dream.

[Pause.] This is where you can always come, to work on your dream. Now, bring in that one idea that will allow you to perfectly create your dream. Let it come through now. [Pause.]

Now you're ready to move into the special place nearby that is just for relaxing. As you enter this area, pay close attention to the colors, the sounds, the smells, the feelings. [Pause.] What kind of furniture will you place here? How will you design the walls and floor and windows? [Pause.] Add anything you like to enhance its beauty and comfort. How about a beautiful bouquet of flowers? Light a candle? Magnificent music? A hot tub? [Pause.]

Sit down, and see yourself resting and relaxing as never before in your life. You feel your energy returning and building—here, your vitality is restored to one hundred percent, and you feel wonderful. [Pause.]

Now your time in your Dream Workshop is drawing to a close. As you prepare to leave, sense all those feelings you have experienced here—the love, the comfort, the safety, the certainty, the warmth, the power of creating everything just as you want it. [Pause.] Know that you can always come back at any time, and you can change it any way you want, at any moment.

Now you move toward the opening, and pass through the entry. The radiant light is there once again, surrounding and permeating you. You pause for a moment to soak up its warmth. [Pause.] Then slowly, you start back down the small, grassy way to the main road. You pass underneath the spreading branches, and the lights and shadows play on your path.

You are ready, now, to be back in your world, for you have everything you need now. As you move back into your everyday world, you take all your new vitality and new possibilities with you. You know that your Dream Workshop will always be there for you, anytime, anywhere that you choose to use it.

Experience yourself back now, in the room where you began. Give your body a long, easy stretch, and notice any sounds and smells around you. When you're ready, open your eyes. Go to your Dream Book, and write about your experience.

You can use this guided meditation to visualize your dream, restore your vitality, and regain your focus. Use it often. It will be most effective if you personalize your tape recording, tailoring the words to suit your own individual tastes. You can listen to it passively as you enter the meditative state and go to work in your Dream Workshop. With experience, you will discover that your answers really are there for you, and they begin to come with greater and greater ease.

MAKE YOUR EMPOWERING TAPE STILL MORE POWERFUL

Use the other side of the tape to read your belief statements, against a background of inspirational music. Visualize your dream, and paint a verbal picture, so you can listen to these valuable messages any time you feel down or angry or uninspired. You will find that you waste less and less time and energy mired in self-pity, boredom, or scattered thinking, and you can get back on the right track quickly.

ACT AS IF

Now, you are ready to really stretch and expand! You've done it in your imagination; now let's try it out for real. What is your dream? How would your life-style or your way of being change, if you were living your dream right now?

STRETCH INTO NEW POSSIBILITIES

Begin today experiencing yourself in a larger way. Think of something that would be a real stretch for you to try—and go do it. Test drive the car of your dreams, and take a camera along to record the experience. Visit that meditative temple where you wondered if you might discover inner peace, even though you've never been anywhere like it before. Go disco dancing, if that's something you would never have thought of doing before. Take ballet or singing lessons. Go skiing; take flying lessons. It all begins with your decision to expand your possibilities. Make the call to set it up.

Try out for a part in community theater; perform in a local carnival as a clown. Wear a bright red bikini to the beach; go to a fine dress shop and try modeling the outfit that embodies the epitome of your dream. Try on the latest Italian silk jackets—or a tuxedo. Ask someone you would never have thought of approaching to go out with you. Have your hair cut in a style that gives you a radically new image.

Go all out. Even if you feel it's "not *you*" at first, you are expanding your possibilities and freeing yourself from old limiting ideas. Scream the loudest of anyone at the football game, if you've always been shy and reserved. Be shy and reserved, if you've always been flamboyant and carefree. Cry as you've never cried before; laugh hysterically. Yell at the television. Greet strangers with a smile and a friendly word. Make a stupid mistake and acknowledge it publicly, if you've always had to be perfect. Get your act together, if you've always been unruly.

Bring balance into your life—ride a seesaw at the playground. Go skinny-dipping at two o'clock in the morning. Stand up in a crowded meeting and give a persuasive speech stating your controversial opinions. Send your poetry collection off to twenty-three publishers.

Stand up for what you believe, even if you're the only one who believes it. Spend an entire day by yourself, without talking to anyone, if that's something you never do. Take a trip to somewhere you're afraid is too far from home.

Speak in someone else's language even though you're afraid they will laugh at you. Go to a job interview for a position you think is "above" you. Run for political office. Call someone you haven't spoken to in a long time, and talk about your dream. Phone someone you can't stand in your family, and find a way to honestly say you love them. Join a group of people who are already successful in a field you are just entering.

You take it from here. Do any or all of these things, and make up more of your own. Choose the very thing that would be most uncomfortable—and do it. The way to get beyond fear is to confront that which you fear the most. Then the rest seems small in comparison. You always find out that the thing you fear is not the monster you thought it would be.

Grow Beyond Discomfort

I especially love this quote from Florence Scovel Shinn's powerful little book of affirmations, *Your Word Is Your Wand:* "I walk boldly up to the lion on my pathway and find it is a friendly Airedale." Make a list in your Dream Book of all the lions on your pathway. Then begin walking up to them, one by one, and start checking them off your list. What are the uncomfortable experiences you want to grow beyond? *Act as if* you were living your dream.

I DID IT

And here's the biggest stretch of all: for *everything that happens, take ownership*. Can you find an argument to challenge this, and an excuse to get around it? Undoubtedly. Richard Bach tells us, "Argue for your limitations, and sure enough, they're yours" (*Illusions*, p. 75). But once your life becomes about you being true to who you are, and telling your truth dauntlessly—the minute you take ownership—no one and nothing else has power over you. The powerful person, the manipulator—no one is ever controlling you. You, and not outside people, places or things, are the sole shaper of your reality.

There's a wonderful quote from *A Course in Miracles*:

> I am responsible for what I see.
> I choose the feelings I experience.
> And I decide upon the goal I would achieve.
> And everything that seems to happen to me,
> I ask for, and receive as I have asked.

You can try this and discover the amazing results. Your perception may be forever changed.

Dream Work Checklist

- Review your Dream Book. Summarize your progress so far.

- Acknowledge yourself!

- Create a support team.

- Shift from *I have to . . .* to *I get to. . . .*

- Study and update complete items, and answer the questions about them.

- Stay current in all communications and responsibilities.

- Eliminate excuses.

- Complete all incomplete items.

- Expose any hidden agendas, and practice developing your new image, true to your real self.

- Take a toothbrush to your life.

- Create and use the chart of belief statements. Read these over morning and evening, and keep them always in your thoughts.

- Write your major life shift.

- Create your own Dream Workshop tape, and use it often.

- Create a belief statements tape.

- Act As If.

- Make a fear list.

- Confront your "lions."

- Try something scary every day. Stretch your ideas of what you can do.

- Everything that happens, take ownership for your experience of it.

7

Keeping the Dream Alive

> Life is a daring adventure, or nothing.
>
> —Helen Keller

FROM DREAM TO REALITY, this has been an adventure. And this is only the dawn in your future of dream living. Look at what you have become in the process of building your dream. The face you now see in the mirror is the image of an empowered being. Your fears have faded, replaced by a sparkling new motivated personality. You *are* your dream.

To keep creating tomorrows filled with happiness, achievement, accomplishment and satisfaction, begin in this moment saying what you want and rewarding yourself for every thought and act you take to bring it about. Exercise determination to shift your energy whenever your thoughts and actions take a turn away from actively supporting your dream.

Stretch until your comfort zone *encompasses* living your dream. People who arrive at this stage frequently report that, as their dream is more and more a part of their daily reality, abandoning it is harder than moving forward. Avoiding making the call is more difficult than facing the possibility of rejection and *just doing it*.

Just do it will become the slogan of the moment when you have made the firm decision to live your dream.

When new dreams come along, begin a Dream Board without delay. And be a courageous dreamer.

Living your dream is simple—but not always easy. All it takes is for you to decide that's what you're going to do, no matter what. Give yourself a standing, gold-embossed personal invitation:

You Are Cordially Invited
To the Event of Your Lifetime

*   *   *

Live Your Dream

Become All You Can Be
Achieve All You Are Capable of Achieving
Fulfill the Ultimate Purpose of Your Life

- - - - - - -

Come As You Are
Time: Starting Immediately
Place: Right Where You Are
Please Bring: The Best of Yourself

R.S.V.P. – A.S.A.P.

Throughout the book I have encouraged you to go back and review work you have done previously and thoughts you have had about previous experiences. Reviewing what has happened and learning to think about things in a new way, are important to assure that you keep growing to new levels instead of just repeating old patterns. We keep our old programmed perceptions until we make a conscious decision to see things differently.

Examining and questioning our perceptions may draw us into a whirlpool of fear, anger and guilt. But by moving through it, we come out on the other side with the freedom to let go of faulty thinking, choose new thoughts more in alignment with our dreams, and release our own inner creativity. And by reviewing your successes and the progress you have made, you give yourself valuable reinforcement. You come to appreciate clearly *how* you have created exactly what you wanted. You are a powerful creative being! When you choose to create your dream—and keep choosing that—you can have it!

So, as a brief summary of the "Live Your Dream" process, the steps to take are: first, ask always—*what do I want?* Decide to live your dream. Take a look at your beliefs, values and habits, and replace old ones with new ones that will empower you. Define the steps and specify dates for completing your dream work. Design your life to motivate and support your new dream and your new values and goals. Turn whatever happens into an opportunity for growth: find the gift, and look for the learning. Keep stretching beyond limited ideas of what you can do. And finally, get support from others, and support yourself with your Dream Book work and by using the techniques introduced in this book. In other words:

- Define the dream.

- Clear away obstructions and be clear about your dream.

- Cultivate a winning attitude.

- Take inventory and take charge.

- Turn negatives into positives.

- Dare to stretch and expand.

- Do the work to keep the dream alive.

STAYING ON TRACK

As you move into the culminating lap of your current "Live Your Dream" cycle, here are some questions designed to bond your progress firmly in place. Write the answers in your Dream Book.

- What makes my heart sing?

- In what ways has the definition of my dream changed since I began reading this book?

- What is my Dream Statement now?

- What is the most important thing I have learned about myself from writing in my journal?

- What new habits lead me to realize my dream?

- What new beliefs are making my dream a reality?

- What changes in me have resulted from my work on completing things?

- What remains for me to complete? What is my plan for completing each item I've listed?

- What issues, situations and relationships remain that need to be resolved or dealt with so I can live my dream?

- Who are the people who are empowering me to live my dream today?

- What are the other empowering forces in my life?

- What is the biggest stretch I've made so far?

- What additional stretches will I make?

- What is the single most important thing I need to do to keep myself on track with realizing my dream?

- What clues can I pick up from my mood or thought patterns to help me notice when I am or am not living my dream?

- What are the greatest personal rewards I receive from living my dream?

WRITING IN YOUR DREAM BOOK IS THE ANSWER— WHAT IS YOUR QUESTION?

Much of the work you have been doing has been designed to move you beyond the problem-solving morass, on to the *creative process*. So rather than "paralysis through analysis," you bring change through taking action. Rather than tackling your problems one by one, within the old structure and format that limited you in the first place, you can step out beyond where you are, and *create a new reality*.

Writing in your Dream Book is one of the most valuable self-help tools you can use, as you choose to model your life in the direction you want it to go. Over the years, clients and friends have often joked about me: "No matter what's going on in your life, Joyce will suggest that you write about it." It's true. No one else can answer your questions with the truth that comes from *your* heart. Do you recall the line from Shakespeare's *Hamlet*—"To thine own self be true"? The direction you receive from within is the most genuine direction you can receive.

So many people have warmly acknowledged, "By your encouraging me to keep a Dream Book, my life is completely different now. It works!" No other way provides such a powerful means of integrating past experiences and using these insights to mold your future. Your Dream Book is your strongest counsel and your truest advisor. It is your therapist, teacher, advocate, confidante and best friend.

The great Nobel Prize-winning physicist Albert Einstein once said that he would begin to worry about mankind if we ever stopped keeping journals.

A successful professional woman named Phyllis wrote the following words about her experience with such writing:

> Scared witless by the strong affirmation of my writing ability at a writers' conference four years ago, I froze. For nearly two years, I could write nothing. Then I heard about Joyce's Journaling for Joy classes. An introductory session convinced me this would be my key, and I joined a weekly group. Now I have eight hundred spiral notebook pages filled to the brim—and more coming. I am nearly ready to prepare my work for publication. The

safe, nonjudgmental environment of this group unlocked doors that had remained closed for so long.

The process has allowed me to be deeply in touch with my feelings. I am so much more aware of everyone and everything around me. The biggest change it's made in my life is that now I am able to *write* my *feelings*. It has put me in touch with the real wellspring of my inner self.

CHOOSE YOUR TOPIC—AND WRITE

There are numerous applications of journal writing—many techniques that may be useful in your future dream work. The following section gives you various topics, so you can look through it at any time and pick the topic that speaks most directly to whatever issue you are dealing with. So:

- Get your Dream Book.

- Find a quiet place.

- Put on some uplifting background music.

- Surround yourself with flowers and scented candles.

- Settle in comfortably.

- Choose whatever topic is important right now.

- Read the discussion about your chosen topic.

- Close your eyes, and let your feelings and thoughts flow.

- When you have an insight, gently open your eyes and write it down.

MY DREAM'S SO BIG—WHERE DO I START?

Write a list of fifty actions you might take to move yourself one step closer to living your dream. Create a cluster diagram, as a visual picture showing how one action might lead to others. Here's a diagram done by a man whose dream was to become instrumental in improving the quality of education in the school his children attended.

ACTIONS TO TAKE

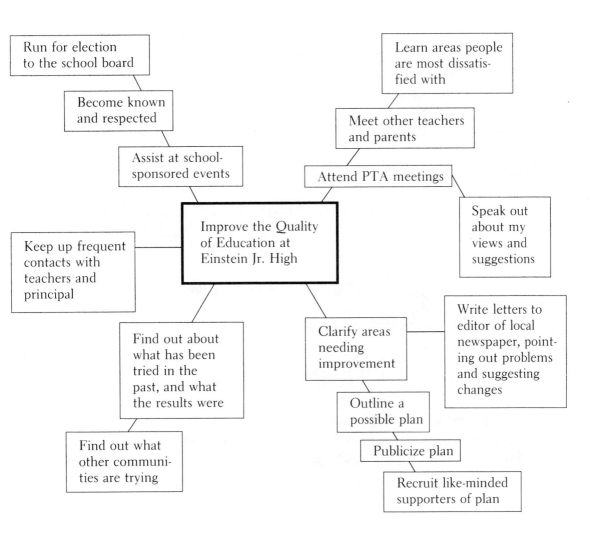

IS THERE A WAY TO DO/HAVE ALL I WANT?

What exactly *do* you want? Write each idea on a single page, and plot your steps for achieving it. Then spread out all your pages in front of you, and consider how they might fit together. Will you pursue several of the goals simultaneously? Does it make sense to finish one before you begin work on another? How much time and effort needs to go into each? What approach will you take? What do you *really* want?

WHY IS IT IMPORTANT TO ME TO LIVE MY DREAM?

Write answers to the following questions:

- What's it going to be like to be a person fulfilling my dream?
- What will the benefits be?
- Who will be empowered by my realizing my dream?
- How will this affect me?

Is your dream large enough to absorb all your energy, to command all your imagination, to use all your resources, and impact the world in an important way? Compare this state of being to just getting by, purposelessly. Why *is* it important to realize your dream?

HOW CAN I BE SURE WHAT MY TRUE GIFTS ARE?

Imagine you have been drifting, lost at sea for several days and not knowing which direction to steer your little lifeboat. Morning dawns, and you see that overnight you have come within view of a tiny tropical island. As you draw near, you recognize it to be the very island where the wise sages you have been seeking reside. You have been searching for answers; you will find them here.

Write your own fantasy story in which your answers are revealed. First, you might like to read the example below, a story that came to me as I was writing my thoughts about someone who was uncertain whether to devote her life to expressing her creative talent.

The woman eyed the men on the shore with some trepidation. A tall, majestic man came over to assist Starr with the docking of her raft.

"We heard you were coming, and we have prepared a place for you," he said. No one seemed affected by her arrival, so Starr followed her newfound guide. Walking among the trees, groups of men were visible, working at various tasks—tanning hides, building rafts, stringing beads.

"What have you come for?" Starr's guide inquired.

"It is time for me to be in the light and to find my gift," she responded. "Who should I talk with?"

"What is it you'd like to know?" he asked.

"I want to know what to do."

Starr's guide said, "You have been given a gift—a gift of creativity. Do not ask *how* or *why*. Just begin. Did you think you would be asked to justify yourself?"

Starr found herself laughing at the ridiculousness of the idea, as her guide reached over and put his arm around her shoulder. He continued, "I will give you my cloak of freedom, and you will then remember." Starr could not believe that only a few moments ago she had felt as if she were in bondage, and out of this new certainty she was now released.

She wondered if she should ask. . . . "I also came with a question for your wise one."

His smile revealed his sparkling white teeth. "First, a bath in the crystal waterfall . . . then on to more truth."

Starr glanced around and found herself alone in the most beautiful secluded spot she'd ever seen. Ferns, trees and flowers of all colors and scents bloomed around a crystal-clear pool fed by a waterfall. She wondered if she was dreaming as she glided into the pool. Feeling supported and lifted up by the water, she floated and paddled around effortlessly.

When she finally emerged refreshed and had pulled her clothes back on, her new friend suddenly reappeared. "Now?" she asked.

"Yes—now," he replied. They walked up a sloping path between two enormous boulders. Looking past her friend, Starr could see an old woman seated on a rock, feeding a deer.

The old woman looked up and smiled. "Why does everyone here seem to love me?" Starr wondered. She said, "Hello. I have a question still in my mind, and yet it does not seem to fit—here."

"Ask it," was the old woman's reply.

"What am I to do about money?"

"Do you *see* it?" the old woman asked.

"Yes."

"Then it's yours. No more darkness. Only light. Choose light."

"And remember my eyes," said her guide with a kindly gaze that reassured Starr she would always be free to follow her heart.

WHAT DO I DO WHEN MY RESPONSIBILITIES ARE DRAGGING ME DOWN?

Most people have been trained to be critical, organized, logical, responsible—not creative. Creativity was that little extra that it was always nice to have, while the main emphasis was on discipline. The focus on *structure* rather than *expression* can easily drag us down. We can, however, with imagination, focus on creative expression while continuing to operate within the required boundaries.

For example, take the way many people approach the festivities of a holiday season. "Ugh!" they groan. "All those gifts to buy and events to plan for. How can I possibly manage all these added demands on my already busy schedule? It gets more overwhelming every year." The (self-imposed) trap is rigid, and the focus is firmly set upon resistance and struggle.

Imagine the alternative approach now: "I just *love* buying presents—the special thought that goes into selecting just the right gift for each individual. Decorating my home, for me, symbolizes decorating my life with my dream. I love expressing myself in this way." This person has chosen an uplifting, creative approach rather than a dragged-down, burdened approach.

What choices are available to the person taking the first approach? That person might: 1) skip celebrating holidays altogether, becoming more honest about his or her true feelings about them; 2) change to the second approach, focusing on the positive instead of the negative aspects of holiday preparations; 3) continue indefinitely having very unpleasant experiences of the festivities.

When you feel dragged down, your choices are the same. Explore what you want by writing at the top of a clean page: What will I change? How can I introduce creativity and flair into my approach to this situation?

A man named Jared wrote the following response to these questions:

> This annual report is always such a chore. How could anyone *enjoy* preparing it? Well, let's see . . . is there *anything* about it that is fun? I know one aspect of it that I really *hate*—the pressure that builds up from leaving it until the last week before the board meeting. That's one thing I sure could change.
>
> Another thing that makes it impossible is trying to get all the facts and figures together from so many scattered, disorganized sources. The process would be much easier if I start out by collecting all the files and having the information I need to work with right at my fingertips.
>
> It's going to be a challenge to change my approach here, though. *Fun?* Well, anything's more fun when I'm doing it with Angela. Wonder if she'd be willing to help? And the new computer spread sheet may make it easier, too. I do like its added capabilities. Maybe I'll try drawing up some special graphics, to spice up the report some.
>
> I know! In the revenue section, I'll create a colorful chart that highlights the benefits of the new sales strategies I introduced last season, and make some further recommendations. Before long, it will be evident to everybody that my ideas could play a much bigger role in making company policy decisions. That is what I really want. Preparing an impressive annual report might be a good idea, after all!

Jared has outlined several changes he will make. He explores his onerous task until he arrives at a way to associate the job with a purpose that is important to him. And he introduced several new ideas for approaching the task with creativity and flair. Note how he has transformed an odious task into a stimulating opportunity in a single, brief writing session!

HOW WILL I HANDLE FEAR?

Pretend that you are hiring an expert to advise you on how to handle your fear. Write a list of questions the expert can be expected to ask you about your fear. These might include:

- What is your fear about?

- What are you afraid of?

- What is the worst possible outcome?

- If your fear is on the surface, what lies underneath?

- Is the fear truly about the present experience, or does it gain power by evoking some related past experience?

- How is your fear protecting you?

- How could you be safe while moving beyond your fear?

- If someone else were telling you about this fear, what advice would you give them?

- What can you do to get out of your fear and into your creativity?

Now, answer the "expert's" questions. Then write fifteen suggestions the expert might give to you, based on the understanding he or she has obtained from your answers.

IS IT ALWAYS GOING TO BE THIS HARD?

Write a "poor me, awful, awful" story, exaggerating your hardship to its extreme, even to the point of humor. Make a cartoon drawing illustrating your plight.

Explore what you mean by "hard." Instead of nonproductive worrying, change your question to: What's it going to take, and am I *willing to do whatever is necessary*? What if there is no "quick fix" available, and you have no choice but to stay with it? What is your realistic assessment of what is required?

HOW CAN I GET RID OF MY ANGER?

Many people today who have done some self-healing work have arrived at an oversimplified conclusion. They say very convincingly to themselves, "What's done is done. I forgive it, I release it, and I let it go." This statement contains the seed of truth, but I find that all too often, it is just not enough. And it can be self-deceptive, as no amount of good intentions can cover up real feelings that remain unexpressed.

Permanently getting rid of our anger usually requires that we get in touch with and express the hurt that lies at its source. When you are ready to release your anger, write this question at the top of a blank page: What's underneath my anger? What is the hurt that needs to be expressed?

You may prefer to begin writing out your anger and your fury or rage. Getting these feelings out in the open may be exactly what you need to do first. Be sure to continue, uncovering the unexpressed pain.

Here is an excerpt from the writing of an angry teenager named Gina. Note how she has used it to work from her anger, to her pain, to her learning.

> I hate it! He can't do this to me! Damn! I won't let him do this to me! He told me he loved me! *Me!* Now he's off with somebody else. And I love him—at least I *thought* I loved him. Maybe

I hate him, now. What a fool I feel like, falling all over him, believing every word he said. Now I find out it all meant nothing! I'm embarrassed in front of my friends. . . . Most of all, I hate to admit to myself I could make such a colossal mistake. I should've known better.

I suppose the signs were there. But I didn't want to see them. I preferred to believe he was just busy, or tired. I *needed* him to love me. That's what hurts. I needed it, and I turned my needing into pretending that he did, giving up my good judgment, and fooling myself.

I *need* to be loved. It hurts to be burned. It hurts to be alone. It's painful to admit my needy feelings.

Crying helps. . . .

There's learning for me here. I'll never betray myself for any guy again! I *don't need* love like that! In fact, I want to *want* love, not *need* it. I can live with myself, but I can't live with fooling myself. That's my truth!

HOW CAN I GO TO SLEEP WITH THESE UPSETTING THOUGHTS ON MY MIND?

The following story unfolded for me as I sat quietly writing an answer to this question:

Once there was a remarkable Indian brave who, from sun passings beyond the far horizons of his memory, was told by his father, "A child is to be kissed and loved before falling into sleep; this is the way of our people."

It was the custom of this boy's tribe that each child, at birth, was presented with an oval-shaped stone with a surface as radiant as the sunlight itself. Peering into it was like seeing through to the depths of a sparkling clear stream unrippled by the faintest sigh of the wind.

This precious stone given to the newborn child was placed in a pouch of the softest leather, to be worn around his neck as an amulet for the duration of his days under the sun and the moon.

Each evening, in the warm glow of the flickering campfire, the father of this infant child would gently remove the stone and examine it closely. Then he would polish away from its surface any blemishes or scratches or smears it might have accumulated during the boy's brush with the forces of pain or hardship he had met with that day. Only when the stone was once again as clear and transparent as the love beaming from his father's eyes was it returned to the leather pouch, a shining companion to accompany the young child into the world of the dream.

As the boy grew in years and experience, he was diligently instructed by his father until, one day, he was judged old enough and trustworthy enough to become the caretaker of his own stone. Never a mar or a scratch was allowed to remain on the stone's surface from one day to the next, and so its interior depths were forever protected from the disturbances of scratch upon scratch.

At the very heart of the stone, a soft pool of light could be seen. From it, the clear, pure, undistorted image of the boy's own soul was reflected back to meet his steady, unfaltering gaze. The brave grew up to be a great, wise chieftain and leader of the people.

The events of a hectic or distressing day can easily mar the surface of your precious stone and cloud your vision of that shining self inside. Scratches and gouges must be polished away each day, to keep your vision from becoming lost or damaged and to preserve the bright, clear image of yourself.

Take your imaginary stone in your hand now, and examine it closely. How would you write your stone's story of this day? What chisels chipped away at your stone's surface today? What hammers pounded at its core? What gouges and blasts did it absorb or fend off? What forces of tension wrenched at it? Draw a diagram of your stone's disfigurement, labeling each incident of distress. Write an accounting of all the disturbances of your stone's day. Write whatever you need to say, to "get it off your chest."

Then, looking at your diagram and reading over your writing, ask yourself: How will I use this? What did I learn? What will I do? On your diagram, mark the action or thought that polishes off the scratch left by each incident of the day.

Conclude by writing a statement for yourself that begins: "Now that my stone is polished once again, I see myself as clear and free. I see. . . ."

WHEN YOU DON'T LIKE THE WAY THINGS ARE

When you don't like the way things are, write about it in your Dream Book. Then go to work on it: How is this *perfect* for me? What am I learning? Don't give up until you can answer these questions in a way that gives you an insight. It may not come right away, and it may be unexpected, but eventually, the insight will always be there.

WHEN YOU FEEL DISSATISFIED

When you feel as if there is something you want and aren't getting in your life, ask yourself what you want. Then write a list of times when you have had that. Ask yourself what patterns are there in your list. Have I been taking action to get what I want lately? What situations must I put myself in, to experience joy (money, fun or whatever it is you want)?

WHAT IF MY PRESENT REALITY DOESN'T MATCH WHAT I WANT?

If you still don't feel at peace with yourself after writing in your journal, ask: do I want to *rewrite* this, to introduce a new sense of peace?

A young boy whose mother was an alcoholic felt devastated by the way his tenth birthday had turned out. After he had written all about it, he was still feeling a great deal of pain. I asked him to write, side by side, the ideal story of how he wished his birthday had turned out. Almost immediately, he realized that his disappointment stemmed from the mismatch between his two stories. He jumped to conclude: "Next year, I think I'll just let my birthday be like any other day. I won't expect so much. Then I won't be so miserable."

This boy had demonstrated an invaluable insight, one that takes many people a lifetime of bitter experience to arrive at: he decided to be responsible for the mismatch between his ideal expectations and the way things were. He was learning to take responsibility for the feelings and thoughts he had about what happened to him, instead of experiencing himself as a helpless victim of circumstance.

Whenever you experience a mismatch between your expectations and the ways things are, first write your feelings about how things are. Then write your ideal scene: what expectations and hopes do you have? Review your two writings and conclude with a summary statement that assumes responsibility for creating what you want.

HOW DO I FIT MY NEW SELF INTO MY EXISTING REALITY?

As you progress toward a fuller and brighter expression of living your dream now, you may find yourself changing faster inside than your environment and the people and circumstances outside you are. While this mismatch may feel frustrating and exasperating, it actually represents just another opportunity to keep focusing on what you want and where you're going. Keep cleaning up, clearing out, and moving forward—realizing that some changes may take longer than others.

Write about the discomfort you're experiencing. How does it feel? What do you feel like doing on impulse? What concrete plans can you make for achieving the result you desire? Review and update your Dream Plan. How are you doing at meeting your projected deadlines?

WHY IS MY PAST SO IMPORTANT?

Can't I just forget it, and get on with my life? This kind of question often surfaces when we come up against some block from the past that is stopping our learning today. Everything about us is based on our past, so the value of uncovering our past is to help us understand our present and release our future from the grip of the past.

Two questions to write about are: What from my past is blocking me from moving forward today? What would I choose to do if there were no blocks? Write a page about "The strengths the past has developed in me"; and "the necessary learning my past has afforded me."

As you learn from your past experiences, allow new questions to surface, continuing to lead to expanded understanding. Simply remain open, write whatever question slips into your conscious awareness, and sit receptively as you allow a response to be formulated, leading to your next insight. The information that bubbles up from your subconscious mind is a vast resource for self-understanding that is always available whenever you invite it to come forward.

WHEN YOU WANT TO HEAL PAST PAINS

Here's an exercise to take this idea further: Write a letter to your mother, father, grandmother, grandfather or whoever took primary care of you as a child. Tell her or him what you would have liked to receive. Create in your letter the exact feelings and experiences you wanted when you were a child.

Paint the picture as if it were actually happening. Let yourself feel what you wanted to feel then—really feel those feelings. You can heal past hurts by replacing them with new pictures in your mind. Imagine your caretaker gently saying to you, "That is exactly what I wanted you to have . . . I really did."

Write a letter to your father or a secondary caretaker or other authority figure, following the same instructions. You need never mail these letters, unless you choose to; the main healing work you will be doing is for yourself and your own memories.

WHEN YOU'RE READY TO COME TO PEACE WITH YOUR PAST

You are a product of all the experiences you have ever had and people you have known—*plus* the thoughts and beliefs you have formed about them.

Your relationship with any significant person or event from your past can be renegotiated today. But, you say, there's so much I just can't remember. I've *tried*, but it was all so long ago. . . . We look for a big flash of enlightenment, but more often, our understanding comes to us in little sparks, once we sit down and start to light the fire.

One effective technique for accessing material from your past is to begin writing stories of your childhood. Write as if you were going through your life as with a picture album. In fact, if you have an old photo album, use it. Write a story about each picture that seizes your attention.

Don't stop with simply writing the story. Read over what you have written, and ask yourself: What did I learn from this person/ event? What am I learning now from this memory? How have these incidents in my past shaped me to be the person I am today? Write your response.

Each time you write, new memories will present themselves— always, I've discovered, at the very moment you are ready to deal with them. Your stories will reveal in a capsulized way the impact each important person in your family and your background had on you. Let your stories lead you to discover the purpose each person had in being in your life; what that person came into your life to assist you in learning.

Whenever you come to a period where you were in conflict with another person or felt misunderstood by someone, follow up your story of it with a parallel story written from *their* point of view, as closely as you can imagine it would be.

You become responsible for your memories when you re-create them. You begin to understand your learning and how these events helped to shape you and your ideas. You make the transformation from the incomplete story to the story that becomes complete and perfect.

WHEN YOU HAVE STRONG FEELINGS

Write in your Dream Book whenever you have strong feelings. Follow up emotional events by recording them and taking a closer look at what was going on. Strong feelings are a vital link to your creative energy, waiting to be released.

Whenever you write in your Dream Book, make it a practice never to stop with just telling the story. Always continue on, and write what your *feelings* are about it. What was the emotion tied to it? How did it make you feel? How did you feel about yourself? If it's an upsetting situation, or if you feel anger or anxiety, be sure to write about that fully. How do you feel now? If you've stirred up some sadness, do you want to just have it for now, or is there some action you need to take? Ask yourself, "What does this writing invite me to do?"

One woman, after writing about her family, exclaimed, "I didn't realize it was going to be so hard! All this anger started bubbling up in me." Who was the anger for? How did it feel? Where was it in your body (always good questions to write about)? "It started right down in my gut, but as it surged upward, it changed into power. I felt there was power coming from inside me."

And when asked what conclusion her writing would lead her to, she replied, "I don't want my father to keep letting me down! I'm finally going to accept that he isn't the person I've been trying to make him be. I've just gotten the message that he doesn't exist only to serve my needs. . . . I guess I was pretty self-centered, not to realize that before now. I'm excited about accepting myself and my father exactly as we are. I can foresee a whole new relationship between us, based on truth instead of fantasy."

HOW CAN I BE POWERFUL WITHOUT BEING OVERPOWERING?

The problem many people have with power is that they confuse power of the spirit with power of the ego. At the level of the ego, we battle to control, dominate and manipulate, based on our fear. At the level of spirit, we simply exist and express ourselves.

Expressing your *spirit* powerfully will usually energize those around you. On the other hand, expressing your *ego* powerfully may make others feel unsafe around you. (And, of course, someone else who is accustomed to expressing his or her ego powerfully in relationship to you may resist your decision to express your spirit. It may be perceived as threatening to the control they have held over you. The balance of your relationship may have to shift.)

Your becoming more creative, more loving, more intuitive, more joyful, expressive, effective, responsible, independent, sure of yourself, direct, dynamic, energetic, free, more true to who you are—stands to benefit others greatly. Do you seek this at the expense of anyone else?

Ask yourself about the perceived threats attached to your power: What is it I seek to express powerfully? Who is threatened? In what ways might I respond to their fear? Can I trust myself to use my power wisely? What will my world be like when I am expressing my power openly and honestly?

HOW CAN I BE NURTURING WITHOUT BEING TAKEN ADVANTAGE OF?

Make sure you're not taking advantage of anyone else. Do you need to be needed? If some part of your self-worth is based on what you're giving to others, then you may be using them. Such a relationship will inevitably be exposed as one of two people taking advantage of each other.

So what is your motive in being nurturing? What do you expect to receive in return? If the other person were to reject you, would it make any difference in your willingness to offer nurturing? If so, then your "nurturing" may not be nurturing at all, but a pact to get what you need, in disguise.

Give nurturing out of your best self, without conditions or anticipation of returns. Do not do what you are not willing to do freely.

Nurturing is a two-way street in healthy relationships. Develop an awareness of the balance of give-and-take in your relationships. A relationship that feels draining is one to take a second look at: what about it induces you to give more than you want to give? What are you "buying," at such an expensive price? Do you choose to maintain that state of affairs? What will you do?

Make a list of people who take advantage of you, or people you suspect may start taking advantage of you. Then make a second list of people you take advantage of. Write about what you need and have tried mistakenly to get from these relationships. Write about how your needs can be met without taking advantage of others. Write how to bring balance and joy into your relationships.

AM I DECEIVING MYSELF?

Write, "If I *were* deceiving myself, what lies would I tell myself?" What is the truth I'd want to avoid knowing? What is the image of myself I want to preserve? What would I have to admit?

Write a character study of yourself, as if it were done by an empathetic friend who truly understands you. Then write at the top of a clean page, "What do I *really* want, and how can I best achieve it?" Write freely any thoughts that come to mind, including objections and "*yes, but*'s." After each objection, return to the question, "What do I really want?"

WHAT ABOUT THE SIDE OF MYSELF I JUST CAN'T STAND?

Draw a picture of yourself, divided down the middle into "the light side" and "the dark side." Write on each side various traits that characterize that side. Then remove each characteristic from the dark side by drawing other people—people in your life you "can't stand"— to project those characteristics onto. (Note that someone who displays a trait you "can't stand" usually represents some aspect of *yourself* that you have been unwilling to acknowledge.)

Now, take your original drawing and cut it in half. (Note that you now have half a person—surrounded by other people you "can't stand.")

Pretend that you are a concerned counselor, and that your task is to interview each of these other "intolerable" people. Sympathetically, question them until you understand what purpose their undesirable characteristics serve. Write the questions you ask, and the answers they give. What reasons do you perceive for their adopting such undesirable characteristics? Write out your recommendations for helping them to be more effective and to love themselves more.

Finally, close your eyes and reclaim each of your "dark side" characteristics. See yourself joining with each of the other "undesirable" persons you have interviewed, and thanking each for the new understanding he or she has given you. See yourself as unified with all these people, and with all of the elements within yourself. Open your eyes, and draw a new picture.

I'M LIVING MY DREAM, BUT I CAN'T PAY MY BILLS

How can I make enough money to support myself, doing just what I love to do? This is a question often asked by people who are beginning to confront the realities of living their dream. Sit down with your Dream Book, and visualize yourself living your dream to the hilt. Ask yourself: What is my predominant need for self-expression? How do I most love to express myself? What part do other people play in the picture? How do others benefit from my living my dream? What are the benefits they would be happy to pay me for? Jot down any other questions that occur to you to be answered as you pursue your dream.

Then ask: Where have I stopped short of what it takes? What more would I have to do, to be completely successful? Where am I, on a time-line of living my dream from beginning to end? What have I accomplished so far, and what remains that I'm going to have to do? Plot these events on a scale that pictures the time-line of your dream.

Is there any part of your dream that is consistent with being irresponsible about paying your bills? Of course not! It would be counterproductive and self-defeating. So what is your transition plan for moving toward living your dream *and* paying your bills—remaining responsible throughout this shift?

HOW DO I GET OUT OF THIS SLUMP?

First ask: Do I *want* to get out of this slump? What's stopping me? Write a dialogue between two characters: the person who *loves* (or at least, has some attachments to) the slump you're in, and the person who is chomping at the bit to get going. What is the first person avoiding? What makes the second person give in to that argument? Let the two characters each debate their positions until a mediator enters, promising them a million dollars if they can arrive at some resolution of their differences that satisfies the needs of both.

To consolidate your learning, make up a slogan or design a saying for a fortune cookie that summarizes your newfound wisdom.

HOW CAN I GET SOMEONE TO CHANGE?

Write a list titled "The behaviors of __(the person's name)__ that cause problems for me." Then next to each, write a list of specific changes you'd like the person in question to make. Write about how your life might be different if the person changed. How would you be affected by these changes? Hwo would *you* be different? How do *you* want to be?

Explore your options, deciding to be the way *you* want to be, *whether or not* the other person changes. Why are you using him or her as your excuse, anyway? Why not drive separately, if being on time is important to you, and the other person is always late? Go ahead and take the workshop they're not interested in—by yourself. Start your diet now; don't wait until they change their style of eating and cooking. Make the decision that *you* choose to put low-calorie foods into your mouth.

Ask yourself, would *you* want to be in a relationship with *you*? Why? Write a list of changes you will make in yourself.

Consider discussing your concerns with the other person. What changes would they like *you* to make? What kind of agreement might be negotiated? Sit down together as each of you writes, "The changes [the other person] can expect me to be making are _____." Post your writing where it will remind you to keep your agreement. Schedule a follow-up meeting in one week to discuss any changes either person wants to make in their agreement and to evaluate your learning so far.

Sylvia was a woman I counseled whose perpetual refrain concerned her mother's interference in her life—and Sylvia was fifty years old. "If she would only leave me alone," Sylvia complained. "If only I could make my own decisions without having to take my mother into consideration. . . ."

When Sylvia came to understand that her decisions had nothing to do with her mother, she began to shift her focus to deciding what *she* wanted to do with her life. Soon she no longer needed to complain—she was too busy. Within a year, Sylvia's mother started a new business of her own, saying, "I guess I'll just have to start living *my* dream, too!" Sylvia was astounded that the changes she made in herself had "magically" precipitated the changes she had started out wanting her *mother* to make.

WILL I HAVE TO LEAVE MY PRESENT RELATIONSHIP?

Write about the following questions:

- Does my current relationship support me in living my dream?
- What's working in my relationship?
- What's not working in my relationship?
- Is my partner aware of my needs and desires?
- Are my needs and desires important in our relationship?
- What do I need in this relationship?
- What is the purpose of our relationship?
- Why does my partner want to be in relationship with me?

- What holds me in this relationship?

- Am I being completely honest with myself and with my partner? If not, what is it that it's time to communicate? What do I want my partner to know?

- If I stay in this relationship, what changes would need to occur in order for me to realize my dream?

- What have I learned from this exercise so far?

Each time you move to a new level of living your dream or expanding your dream, new demands will be made on your relationships. You will either communicate, tell the truth, make needed adjustments and grow, or your relationships will be at risk of becoming outdated and dysfunctional.

Do these questions sound selfish and self-centered? Ah!—that's a wonderful question, because on the surface, it may seem selfish to keep focusing on what *you* want. But at a deeper level, these questions form the foundation for a solidly grounded relationship, in which you don't cheat the person you're with because you're knowing and being yourself. With your own wants and needs satisfied, your energy is freed to share and express yourself with others. The emphasis shifts from being self-*centered* to being self-*actualized.* In such a relationship, each person says to the other, "Oh, I see—you want to do that! What can I do to make it a win for both of us, as I do what I'll be doing to live my dream, also?"

Any relationship can last, I believe, if both persons maintain the desire and the commitment to keep it alive and growing. My relationship with my husband Bob is constantly evolving from one day to the next. It thrives on the continual focus on results and what each of us wants. "What can I do to support you in getting what you want?" is a question we ask each other almost daily. And, of course, shared dreams are incredibly important in a relationship, too.

So use the questions above repeatedly, whenever it's time to rethink the parameters of your relationship. And keep your focus firmly set on results and how to bring them about.

WHEN YOU COULD USE SOME PRAISE

Write a letter to yourself! Be sure to do this whenever you've had a wonderful experience or a magnificent success. Give yourself lavish compliments, and acknowledge your successes. Re-create the glowing feeling you have, and emphasize your effective role in bringing it about. Congratulate yourself for choosing to live your dream fully, and give yourself lots of love. Seal your letter in an envelope, and write on the outside the date or occasion on which you will open and read it—perhaps: FOR [YOUR NAME]. OPEN ON A DAY WHEN YOU COULD USE SOME PRAISE.

IF YOUR DREAM GROWS FAINT

Reading my Dream Statement over whenever my dream begins to feel faded brings back the inspiration and rejuvenating energy I felt when I originally wrote about it. As soon as I review the work I've scheduled for my three-month, six-month and one-year plans, I sit up and realize, "I'd better get busy!"

If your dream is growing faint, go back and read the inspiring sections you have written in your Dream Book about your dream. Then ask yourself, "Is it time to update my Dream Statement or my Dream Plan?"

Write down every demonstration that shows you are living your dream. Share your successes with others. Consciously strengthen your commitment to living your dream by repeatedly writing, "I know I have the desire to live my dream because _____," and completing it with many different answers. Assign yourself to produce one measurable result each day that is part of bringing your dream into reality.

Then, to serve as a rejuvenating reminder, choose a song that captures the excitement of your dream. Get a recording of it, and play it often.

HOW LONG DO I HAVE TO KEEP WORKING
ON MY DREAM?

This is a question I am often asked. I always laugh and reply, "As long as you want to keep bringing your dreams into reality." I encourage people to do whatever works best to keep their dreams alive—take classes, read books, form a support group. To reassess your progress and reaffirm your commitment to living your dream, write about the following:

- What are the signs that I'm experiencing my dream?

- What accomplishments have I achieved in the past six months?

- Which assignments did I avoid?

- What changes am I avoiding making?

- What's the *big* step I haven't taken yet?

- What have I done in the past to revitalize myself?

YOUR DREAM COME TRUE

And now, here's one final writing exercise which is extremely valuable for achieving your dream. Also, it can serve as a revitalizer when you read it over months or years from now.

Write your story! Write the story that pictures you living the dream you have claimed. Take from thirty minutes to an hour and write several pages inyour Dream Book. Include a descriptive setting that portrays you, your feelings, your environment and other involved characters. Make the words draw the pictures for you. Incorporate your goals, values and motivators into your plot, and write a story climax that shows how all the dream work you've done has paid off in wonderful ways. Read your novel to your dream coach and to other significant people in your life whom you can count on to support you in living your dream.

Here's an example, written by a woman named Beverly.

Never had life been more perfect. Each segment of Bev's busy yet carefree schedule ran without a hitch. The dream was now a reality for Beverly, and she savored every moment.

Spiritually alive, she awakened each morning to the sound of the waves rushing to the shore outside her beachfront home and began the day with the meditations she had grown to cherish, prefaced with some inspirational reading. Peaceful moments alone with the munificent Universe were the bulwark of a full, rich day of work and play. Beverly participated in a blend of yoga and walks along the shore to reinforce her connection to the Divine. Reading and following her own inner truth had rounded out the path of spirituality so vital to her balance. It was a bonus, she considered, that she was able to share her love of truth with the rest of her family.

Family . . . the foundation of her reason for joy. Her daughter Kate was in her final year of law school, with an offer already in hand for an apprenticeship in a fine Washington, D.C. law firm. Kelly was enjoying her sophomore year at the small local college and had recently been elected homecoming queen. Kirk, Beverly's son, would soon be graduated from high school with honors, and had already been accepted to both Harvard and Stanford. And although John had joined the family only recently (a "dad" to the children and loving husband to Beverly), his warmth and generous love brightened every day.

Their home was a demonstration of the beauty and serenity felt by each member. An expanse of glass in the living room reflected the sparkle of the California coast. The muted colors of nature decorated the exquisite interior of the sizable home.

Beverly's attention to her physical well-being was evident in her firm, trim body. Daily exercise was the norm. Regular tennis was interspersed with ongoing yoga. Beverly's organized shopping plan had paid off with a well-coordinated closet—the latest fashions accented by tasteful jewels facilitated her desire to always look her best.

The holidays would be filled with family entertaining and

gatherings at the homes of their many friends. All the kids would be home, filling the house with their own friends and their laughter. Christmas week would culminate with a midnight champagne buffet for a host of friends and family. Even now, the decoration process had begun. Fine ornaments and strands of white twinkling lights and pearls rounded out the stately tree, reminiscent of a romantic, Victorian era.

Beverly's mental agility and productivity had been challenged in her job where she was the top producer in a brokerage house. An abundance of money had long since ceased to be her motivation, and she now produced beyond her wildest dreams for the sheer joy of it. Well-earned respect and accolades were the fruits of her commitment and dedication to her dream. And the community work now funded by her firm—because of her diligent persistence—served hundreds of people every week.

Tomorrow was to be such a special day for Beverly and her two closest friends. As a surprise for one friend's birthday, Beverly had arranged for a private jet to fly the trio to San Francisco for a day of shopping, lunch and a new hit play. Champagne, love and laughter would be their watchwords. The expectation of their merriment brought a smile to her face.

And here's another example from a woman named Lynn:

A quiver of exhilaration surged through her, as the rapturous theme of Dvorak's *New World* Symphony rose and enveloped Lynn in its mystical beauty, luring her attention away from the work on her desk, and laying full claim to her imagination. Willingly surrendering to its inspiration, she leaned back in her easy chair and closed her eyes to receive the gift of the music. The beauty of the surrounding room enveloped her, lending an aura of its own to the magic of the moment.

A procession of happy thoughts paraded past her consciousness. The latest manuscript—a brilliant, delightfully humorous, inspirational work—was expertly developed and complete; she would deliver it with pride and confidence the following day, to a meeting with her publisher halfway around the world.

The traveling was always a special part of this work, meeting such engaging and bright people and staying in interesting new places for a few days. Especially when she was able to bring her son Brendan along. Such an amazing child, that delightful boy, curious and eager to learn about everything, so intelligent and so much fun. And other times when her new beau would accompany her: the delight of going exploring together, of discovering beauty beyond the ordinary, insights into each other from a new perspective, the mutual support given and received in the intimate way that is possible when two people communicate openly and fully out of love.

And the traveling was but a small part of Lynn's ever-enriching life. Probably more than anything else, she loved the opportunity of bringing love into the lives of the many people whose appreciation for her work had brought her so many rewards. She glanced up fondly at the bookshelf of best-selling books she had written. It was a satisfying contribution to make to the world. She could only feel thankful for the guidance she'd received in realizing her utmost potential. The endowments and gifts she sent to organizations doing wonderful work represented being able to give back a small part of what she had received.

As the final strains of the symphony died down, Lynn roused herself from her reflections. A brief stroll through her flower garden, before she would eagerly resume writing. The next project was rapidly taking shape.

Your own story may be longer or shorter than these examples. You can add to it as your vision and your dream grow. Be sure to describe all the various aspects of the dream life you envision: career, self-expression, relationship, finances, home, family, recreation, etc.

Set aside time for reading and updating your story on New Year's Day every year.

*   *   *

Five-year-old Cathy, who had come into the shoestore knowing exactly what kind of shoes she wanted, asked the salesperson, "Do you

know *everything* about shoes?" The reply was, "Well, sort of...."
Cathy asked incredulously, "Then *why* are you selling them?" The
salesperson stepped back and allowed herself to hear an important
message: If you are living your life by "sort of's," what *sort of* result
can you expect?

Will you be the main character in your own life? Will your life be
a daring adventure, or nothing?

This is your life! Now that you have finished this book, go right
back and start again. Experience shows that the person who grows is
the one who starts the process all over again as soon as they have
reached the goal of one dream.

See it! Create it! Claim it! Celebrate it!

Suggested Reading List for Enjoyment and Expansion

Allen, James. *As a Man Thinketh*. Sun Publishers, 1983.

Andrews, Lynn V. *Jaguar Woman*. Harper & Row, 1986.

Assagioli, Roberto. *Act of Will*. Penguin, 1974.

_____. *Psychosynthesis*. Penguin, 1971.

Bach, Richard. *Illusions: The Adventures of a Reluctant Messiah*. Delacorte, 1977.

Baer, Jean. *How to Be an Assertive (Not Aggressive) Woman in Life, Love, and on the Job: A Total Guide to Self-Assertiveness*. New American Library, Signet Books, 1976.

Beattie, Melody. *Codependent No More: How to Stop Controlling Others and Start Caring for Yourself*. Hazelden, 1988.

Blanchard, Kenneth, and Spencer Johnson. *The One Minute Manager*. Berkley, 1987.

Bloomfield, Harold, and Leonard Felder. *Making Peace with Your Parents*. Random, 1983.

Bowers, Barbara. *What Color Is Your Aura? Personality Spectrums for Understanding and Growth*. Pocket Books, 1989.

Branden, Nathaniel. *How to Raise Your Self-Esteem*. Bantam, 1987.

Brenner, Paul. *Health Is a Question of Balance*. DeVorss, 1980.

Briggs, Dorothy Corkille. *Celebrate Your Self*. Doubleday, 1977.

Buzan, Tony. *Use Both Sides of Your Brain*. E. P. Dutton, 1983.

Capacchione, Lucia. *The Creative Journal: The Art of Finding Yourself.* New Page Books, 1989.

Cole-Whittaker, Terry. *What You Think of Me Is Non of My Business.* Oak Tree Publications, 1982.

Dass, Ram. *Journey of Awakening: A Meditator's Guidebook.* Bantam, 1982.

Davis, et al. *Relaxation and Stress Reduction.* New Harbinger, 1982.

Dychtwald, Ken. *Bodymind.* J.P. Tarcher, 1986.

Dyer, Wayne W. *Choosing Your Own Greatness.* Nightingale-Conant, 1989.

____. *Your Erroneous Zones.* Avon, 1977.

Ferguson, Marilyn. *The Aquarian Conspiracy: Personal and Social Transformation in the 1980s.* J.P. Tarcher, 1987.

Fields, Rick; Taylor; Weyler; and Ingrasci. *Chop Wood, Carry Water: A Guide to Finding Spiritual Fulfillment in Everyday Life.* J.P. Tarcher, 1984.

Foster, Steven, and Meredith Little. *The Book of the Vision Quest: Personal Transformation in the Wilderness.* Prentice-Hall, 1988.

Foundation for Inner Peace. *A Course in Miracles.* Foundation for Inner Peace, 1985.

Fox, Emmet. *The Mental Equivalent.* Unity School of Christianity, 1984.

Fromm, Erich. *The Art of Loving.* Harper & Row, 1974.

Gawain, Shakti. *Creative Visualization.* New World Publishers, 1978.

Gillies, Jerry. *Moneylove.* Warner Books, 1979.

Goldberg, Natalie. *Writing Down the Bones: Freeing the Writer Within.* Shambhala Publications, 1986.

Haas, Robert. *Eat to Win: The Sports Nutrition Bible.* New American Library, 1985.

Hanley, John. *Lifespring: Getting Yourself from Where You Are to Where You Want to Be.* Simon & Schuster, 1989.

Hesse, Hermann. *Siddhartha.* Bantam, 1982.

Hoffman, Bob. *No One Is to Blame: Getting a Loving Divorce from Mom and Dad.* Science & Behavior, 1979.

Holmes, Ernest. *The Science of Mind.* Dodd, Mead & Co., 1938.

Houston, Jean. *The Possible Human: A Course in Extending Your Physical, Mental, and Creative Abilities.* J. P. Tarcher, 1982.

Huang, Chung-Liang Al. *Quantum Soup: A Philosophical Entertainment.* Dutton, 1983.

Jampolsky, Gerald G. *Love Is Letting Go of Fear.* Bantam, 1982.

Jeffers, Susan. *Feel the Fear and Do It Anyway.* Harcourt Brace Jovanovich, 1987.

_____. *Opening Our Hearts to Men.* Fawcett, 1989.

Johnson, Spencer. *One Minute for Myself: How to Manage Your Most Valuable Asset.* Avon, 1987.

Josefowitz, Natasha. *Is This Where I Was Going?* Warner, 1983.

_____. *Paths to Power: A Woman's Guide from First Job to Top Executive.* Addison-Wesley, 1980.

Josefowitz, Natasha, and Herman Gadon. *Fitting In: How to Get a Good Start in Your New Job.* Addison-Wesley, 1988.

Joy, W. Brugh. *Joy's Way.* J. P. Tarcher, 1979.

Keyes, Ken, Jr. *The Hundredth Monkey.* Vision Books, 1982.

Klauser, Henriette A. *Writing on Both Sides of the Brain: Breakthrough Techniques for People Who Write.* Harper & Row, 1986.

Kubler-Ross, Elisabeth. *On Death and Dying.* Macmillan, 1970.

Lama Foundation Staff. *Be Here Now.* Crown, 1971.

Lenz, Marjorie, and Marjorie Hansen Shaevitz. *So You Want to Go Back to School.* McGraw, 1977.

Lerner, Harriet Goldhor. *The Dance of Anger: A Woman's Guide to Changing the Patterns of Intimate Relationships.* Harper & Row, 1985.

MacLaine, Shirley. *Out on a Limb.* Bantam, 1983.

Maltz, Maxwell. *Psycho-Cybernetics.* Pocket Books, Inc., 1983.

Mandino, Og. *The Greatest Miracle in the World.* Bantam, 1983.

Millman, Dan. *Way of the Peaceful Warrior: A Book That Changes Lives.* H. J. Kramer, 1984.

Noble, Vicki. *Motherpeace: A Way to the Goddess Through Myth, Art and Tarot.* Harper & Row, 1982.

Norwood, Robin. *Women Who Love Too Much: When You Keep Wishing and Hoping He'll Change.* J. P. Tarcher, 1985.

Peck, M. Scott. *The Road Less Traveled.* Touchstone Books, Simon & Schuster, 1980.

Pelletier, Kenneth R. *Mind As Healer, Mind As Slayer: A Holistic Approach to Preventing Stress Disorders.* Peter Smith, 1984.

Phelps, Stanlee, and Nancy Austin. *The Assertive Woman.* Impact, 1975.

Ponder, Catherine. *The Dynamic Laws of Prosperity.* DeVorss, 1985.

Prather, Hugh. *A Book of Games: A Course in Spiritual Play.* Doubleday, 1981.

Prather, Hugh, and Gayle Prather. *A Book for Couples.* Doubleday, 1988.

Price, John Randolph. *The Superbeings.* Fawcett, 1987.

Ray, Sondra. *I Deserve Love.* Celestial Arts, 1987.

_____. *Loving Relationships.* Celestial Arts, 1980.

Shaevitz, Marjorie Hansen. *The Superwoman Syndrome.* Warner, 1985.

Shaevitz, Morton H., and Marjorie Hansen Shaevitz. *Making It Together: As a Career Couple.* Houghton Mifflin, 1980.

Shinn, Florence Scovel. *Your Word Is Your Wand.* DeVorss, 1978.

Siegel, Bernard S. *Love, Medicine and Miracles.* Harper & Row, 1986.

Silva, Jose, and Philip Miele. *The Silva Mind Control Method.* Pocket Books, 1978.

Simonton, Carl, et al. *Getting Well Again.* Bantam, 1982.

Stoddard, Alexandra. *Living a Beautiful Life: Five Hundred Ways to Add Elegance, Order, Beauty and Joy to Every Day of Your Life.* Avon, 1988.

Szekely, Edmond B. *Creative Work: Karma Yoga.* IBS International, 1973.

Teilhard de Chardin, Pierre. *Phenomenon of Man.* Harper & Row, 1965.

Thoreau, Henry David. *The Journal of Henry D. Thoreau.* Princeton University Press, 1984.

Toben, Bob, and Fred A. Wolf. *Space-Time and Beyond (Physics Explains the Unexplainable).* Dutton, 1982.

Tver, David F., and Howard F. Hunt. *Encyclopedic Dictionary of Sports Medicine (Advanced Industrial Technology Series).* Routledge Chapman & Hall, 1986.

Watts, Alan W. *This Is It.* Random, 1972.

Woititz, Janet G. *Adult Children of Alcoholics.* Health Communications, 1983.

Wonder, Jacquelyn, and Priscilla Donovan. *Whole-Brain Thinking: Working from Both Sides of the Brain to Achieve Peak Job Performance.* Ballantine, 1985.

JOYCE CHAPMAN, M.A., is a speaker, teacher, coach, and motivational leader. Through her consulting firm and workshops she provides services for individuals, groups, and companies nationwide. Chapman's work focuses on enabling people to develop their highest potential. Her "Live Your Dream" workshops form the basis for this book. Her background includes 18 years as a teacher and teacher trainer in the California public school system, and a master's degree in Counseling Psychology. She has been happily married for 47 years and is the mother of four grown children and grandmother of 11.

Through her company, Live Your Dream, Joyce Chapman makes available corporate and private consulting/coaching services. For information on workshops, speaking engagements, and individual consultations, write to:

Live Your Dream
826 Orange Avenue, PBM 111
Coronado, CA 92118

or visit: www.joycechapman.com